DEAD IN THE WATER; FOREVER AWAKE

Steph Young

Copyright © 2015 Stephen Young
All rights reserved

Introduction

Hundreds of young men; vanishing without a trace, only for many of them to be found dead; weeks or months later, in remote rivers or creeks, shallow ponds or canals, in areas that search parties have searched multiple times before; their bodies later discovered there, as though placed to be found.

There is something very sinister happening to college-age men. It has been going on since the early '90's, and quite likely since before then. What's more, it isn't stopping; it appears to be escalating, and no-one knows why.

Young men attending college are going missing; the numbers are rising, as they disappear in what can only be described as sinister and inexplicable circumstances. Then they are found dead; always in water, often very shallow water.

"The naughty boys, well....they go directly into the shallow water. And then, they are all gone...no ghost, no memories...as if they never lived in the first place. And then they stay there; awake and afraid."

"The evil is rampant and deep and widespread. He was tortured, taken to the river and killed. Then his body was 'positioned' and taken to a different part of the water."

"Nobody will speculate on the disappearances because they don't understand the sinister nature of the world they are living in. This is dark alchemy indeed."

"Once so vital, he is now…..grist for the mill. For a machine…..A machine full of teeth he never saw coming."

"We take what we need and leave. Understand this: This is necessary. Life feeds on life feeds on life feeds on death feeds on life."

"If people knew the depth of this, they would be terrified to be outside at night, whether out in the country or in the city."

Table of Contents

Introduction 2

Chapter 1: Sinking Into The Ocean 5

Chapter 2: Current Day - Cryptic Clues 25

Chapter 3: The Beginning 52

Chapter 4: Personal Interest 73

Chapter 5: Patterns And Links 80

Chapter 6: The Phone Calls 96

Chapter 7: The Suspects 124

Chapter 8: The Possibilities Continue 156

Chapter 9: Near Misses 177

Chapter 10: Something Getting Into Their Heads ... 211

Chapter 11: Things Get Even Darker 223

Chapter 12: Not Afraid of Death 271

Conclusion 284

Chapter 1:
Sinking Into The Ocean

"By the time you read this message I'll be sinking into the ocean ...ending my time in this wretched life. On this day I can finally see the ones I've seeked all these years. Finally Toader Cazazu can..."

This was the last post on Toader Cazacu's facebook. At the time of writing this book, in February 2016, to the shock of his friends who had seen him just thirty minutes prior to him posting this message on facebook, Toader is missing. He has not posted anything since, and his fate is not known. Is it strange that he used his full name?

Could Toader's message about sinking into the ocean, tie in with what could be construed as a taunting message in a forum, even though the message was posted years before? It was posted from a Japanese i.p. address; perfect for concealing a person's true location, and was posted in response to a thread trying to solve the mystery behind the ever growing number of young men who are being found dead in the water.

"Can't believe I missed this for 4 years! Your theory is sound; too bad all of that work for nothing. Slight problem; just like the night good ol' Jack got two in one night and was almost caught; work unfinished. Alchemy? Transcendence of the

soul/spirit/consciousness. My brother Germain has seen the hypocrisy, the pure greed and the lies conveyed at Nicea. We take what we need and leave. Understand this: This is necessary. Life feeds on life feeds on life feeds on death feeds on life. We will never leave; just sink back to where we came from :)"
Is this a joke? Or, does it hold vital clues? It's something we will look deeply into as this book progresses.

Two hours away, and one day before Toader posted his message on facebook about 'sinking into the ocean,' Harvard student Zachary Marr disappeared while out with his cousins at a Bar in Boston. He was not allowed back into the Bar after going outside for a cigarette. The Bar dispute this. Again at the time of writing, the police released a statement saying that they believe the surveillance cameras show him as he enters the ice cold Charles River. It was a cold night in Boston, in February. Why would a young man go down to the River and get into the water? He had only gone outside the Bar to have a quick cigarette.

In that same stretch of water, two weeks before Zachary disappeared, Matthew Genovese also disappeared after leaving a bar. His co-workers, who were in the bar with him, said that he did not appear to be intoxicated. On January 23rd, 2016, Matthew was found dead in the Hudson River. Strangely, his billfold was found on the pier beside the water.

24 days before this, on December 31st, the body of Northeastern University Dennis Njoroge was found in the river. He had disappeared on November 29th. His body was found in Boston's Charles River on December 31st. Following autopsy and toxicology tests, the city coroner concluded that it was impossible to determine if the young man had drowned by accident or suicide, or if he had "somehow died elsewhere," and was then placed in the water already dead.

The cause and also the manner of the young man's death was therefore listed as "unknown" and the Boston police stated that they were not going to be investigating it. It was determined by them not to be suspicious; despite the fact that from the Coroner's report, he could quite easily have been killed and then placed in the water.

Again in Boston, on February 8, 2014, graduate Eric Munsell was out celebrating his birthday. Eric was in a bar with friends when he was thrown out by a bouncer because, according to his Mother, he had tripped on his way to the bathroom. His body was discovered in the river two months later, at the same spot he was believed to have entered the water, according to cell phone records. A passer-by had seen his "non-viable" body floating in the water. Why had his body not been seen before? Had he been in the water for 2 months, or not?

On Christmas day 2015, the body of Lehman College student Anthony Urena was found dead in the same stretch of water. It was believed his body had drifted from the Harlem River, into the New Jersey side of the Hudson River, where he was recovered. He had last been seen leaving a nightclub in New York City around 5 a.m. He had been missing for six weeks. At this point in time, it is not known if he had been in the water the entire time; or "elsewhere" for some of the time he had been missing.

Indiana student Joseph Smedly was found dead in the water in Griffy Lake, north of Bloomington, on October 2nd, 2015. He'd written on his twitter account; 'If I am found dead; *it won't be suicide*. Perhaps I have said too much." The official autopsy said that he had committed suicide. His sister says he was drowned, with rocks inside the backpack that was strapped to his body when he was found.

Henry McCabe was found partially submerged in a remote body of water on November 2nd, 2015. He had disappeared on Labor Day, September 7th, 2015, in Minnesota. On the night he disappeared, he left what can only be described as the most haunting, most chilling, and most harrowing voicemail, after he went missing. He is screaming, pleading and growling in raw, animalistic agony. Disturbingly, in the background, is something that sounds mechanical. Even more horrific, a voice then interrupts his screams and calmly tells him, in a cold, emotionless, detached voice, "Stop it."

He was found in the water seven miles from where he was last known to have been on the night he disappeared. His body bore no signs of trauma; and yet it had sounded as though he was being tortured. How does that make any sense? What could have been happening to him on that terrible night?

His Mother says, "This is what they did to my son. Someone killed my son. Before Henry died, he was pleading to someone who dropped him in the dark... Henry paid for you to learn the lesson... When he got off from that car in that morning, he had no idea that he was going to die..."

She seems to be suggesting here that Henry was 'delivered' to his terrible fate; as though he was offered up in some form of sacrifice, in some form of pre-planned killing. Rather bizarrely however, the police, despite his harrowing blood-curdling voicemail, say that they do not think there was any foul play involved. He had been missing for 5 days.

An elder in the Twin Cities' Liberian community, of which Mr McCabe was one, commented, "He can't have got here all by himself," to a location that he pointed out is very isolated, very remote, and dark after 6 pm. "Someone dropped him in the water." The Elder made the statement that the police should not overlook the possibility that his death was connected to violence in his home country, where he had endured a life enmeshed in more than a decade of civil war. On the other hand, his death bears remarkable and uncanny similarities to the many other young men being found drowned, who have not come from Liberia to America; who were all-round 'All American' boys....And many of them also made very disturbing phone calls just before they died or were taken, and were then found dead, days or weeks later, in bodies of water. What is perplexing, and very worrying, is that none of these cases are being investigated as suspicious.

We have the terrible case of Walton Ward. His sister says her brother also died in inexplicable, mysterious and terrible circumstances.

"Walton was last seen alive at Landsharks Bar, Indianapolis, with a 'bouncer' at approximately 1:20-1:30 a.m. on October 12, 2012. His last attempt to save his own life was at 1:30 a.m. when he dialled 911 from his Phone for help. His killers interrupted his 911 call and murdered him...He knew he was going to be killed. His desperate call lasted for 1 second, which was just enough to register to the nearest cell phone tower...but it wasn't not long enough to save his life."

"That was the last time we know him to be alive, until construction workers discovered his body on October 22, floating in the River a few blocks from the bar 10 days after his desperate call to 911 on that night. His phone was found on the bank of the River behind a Restaurant. The police said he must have been 'drunk', 'fallen in' or 'gone swimming' in the dead of winter."

Interviewed by crime writer, Eponymous Rex of the Killing Killers Blog Spot, his mother said,
"Where he was found, the depth was just two feet. My conclusion is someone, (probably more than one) was with him. It's very suspicious and illogical that a very healthy, strong, trained athlete 'fell' and drowned in three feet of water on his own."

Other victims, who have ended up dead, the same way, have left comments on their facebook or twitter accounts, that also clearly cry out for investigation. Whether overtly or cryptically, some of these victims are in need of help even before they have disappeared. Something very strange, very alarming, and very sinister is going on.

Why did one young man write this on his facebook page, within hours of his death?
"Not afraid of death cause I'm so curious of what's next."
The answer may not be the most obvious one, as we will later examine. It was the last post on Mason Cox's facebook page. A week later, his body was found in a river, along with the body of his best friend. It was officially classified as 'accidental drowning.' Both autopsies determined that they had died from "accidental drowning compounded by hypothermia,"

according to Sherry Lang, spokeswoman for the Georgia Medical Examiner.

His Mother however, has a different version. "My son was beaten, teeth missing, blunt trauma to the back of his head. His eyes so horrible... His stomach black and blue."

As one victim said before he died, "When you really look into the mystery and the place and the settings and the symbolism, you're f...d, yeah .....It's far too upsetting. Far too unknown."

It's not known explicitly if he was referring to these deaths; however, something was clearly troubling him, something which had led him to seek mental health assistance for the first time in his life, just days before he disappeared. Why did this student, Jake Nawn, make a video in which he says these words, and post it on his facebook, just days before he was found dead in a river near his Plymouth State Campus on November 17th, 2015.

Was he talking about something an outside observer could not understand; about a harmless topic only known by his friends? Or, was he hinting at some kind of desperate trouble he had unwittingly got himself into?

As will later be explored; there are themes here which quite possibly point to more than just a human hand in these disappearances and deaths. Something that is quite possibly so dark, so arcane and alchemical, that it belongs in the realm of rituals which go back centuries. Something that belongs in a dimension of the darkest black magic; and yet something that runs from the lowest echelons to the highest. A slick operation of willing accomplices, lured into a pact which seeks to serve only their higher masters. Allegiances run deep and for now, they remain unbroken.

Jake vanished inexplicably when he had been due to meet his family after class. It was to be five days until searchers spotted his body in the water of the Pemigewasset River. His autopsy determined that he had drowned, although the coroner said, "the exact manner of death will remain undetermined."

In 2011, Mike Shaw wrote of the grief, the anger and the sense of helplessness he felt because he could not save his best friend.
"Sly McCurry did not walk out onto the ice of Lake Superior (Wisconsin) that cold January (2010) winter night and fall through and drown. He was murdered. No one can ever convince me it was anything but murder. He was more than a friend to me. His smile would light up a room. He was always full of life, always happy. He would never have went from the Nightclub to that secluded area alone in 20 degrees below weather, with no coat, and drown. He had no car and after being thrown out of the club via the back

door, on the alleged grounds that he was drunk, he was left in the alleyway. Four months later, his body was found in the lake. I was a trained fighter for many years and felt protective over my friends. I have never received closure. His death was ruled "accidental due to cold water immersion." His scent stopped at the back door of the hotel. Like clockwork, I see this killers strike all over the North-East."

College boys are going missing; later to be found drowned. Not all have drowned in the water; some have drowned elsewhere. According to Ret'd NYPD Kevin Gannon, "They have been abducted, held sometimes for an extended amount of time, mentally tortured, killed, and then placed in the water."

"The evil is rampant and deep and widespread. He was tortured, taken to the river and killed. Then his body was 'positioned' and taken to a different part of the water," says one of the victim's mothers.

The victim type is almost always the same; athletic, popular, high achieving white male college students who go missing after a night out drinking with friends. Choosing to go home, instead of walking back with friends later, or more often, being 'kicked out' of bars, on what later appear quite possibly to be fabricated reasons; they then disappear, only to be found some time later, drowned in nearby rivers or creeks or ponds; even retention tanks.

Many will say they were drunk and disoriented and fell in the river. Many will say inevitably, that the reason they are all of a similar victimology is because more young men than women would choose to walk off alone at night. They will say that they are popular college kids who are letting off steam, drinking too much, and then underestimating how much they have drunk, and as a result they get into difficulty when walking home.

Others however, will ask why they would choose to walk away from their direct route home, often for a long distance, to a river or creek or shallow pond, usually in the middle of winter, without coats, and 'go for a swim' or 'fall in,' rather than go straight home. This is the same scenario for almost all of the victims.

The majority of them were former lifeguards, or on swim teams, well-built and in excellent shape, many excelling as athletes as well as academics; and most of them were not known to be particularly heavy drinkers. They were all highly intelligent, and understandably not prone to jumping onto rivers and lakes in freezing temperatures, on their own, late at night, miles away from home.

Hundreds of young men vanishing without a trace, only for many of them to be found dead, weeks or months later, in remote rivers or creeks, shallow ponds or canals; or in rivers very close to where they were last seen, in areas that search parties have thoroughly searched many times before; their bodies then discovered as though placed there to be found.

Boys are disappearing on the same day across different states, even different countries. There is never any sign of a struggle. There are never any signs of foul play. They are often seen in the presence of unknown strangers, often young, prior to their vanishing.

Always men, always high achievers, always excellent swimmers, always in the colder months. Almost all are kicked out of bars, purposely separated from their friends, made vulnerable and alone and left to their fate.

Why are young men being found drowned, either in water that is only a few feet deep? Or found in remote bodies of water, in areas that the young men would never have been heading to? Some are even found in areas one would think are completely inaccessible.

On October 7, 2010, officials confirmed that they had recovered the body of missing Western University Student Dwight Clark, who had vanished 12 days earlier after leaving a party at around 2 a.m. He was discovered about 1 km from the party, in a log lagoon, which was gated and locked. His friends said he did not appear drunk when he left.

Why and how would he have got into that private property in the first place? Oddly, a blank message was sent from his phone, shortly after he disappeared. The location the message came from was an entirely different location to the one he was found in.

The official story from law enforcement is always that they have 'accidentally drowned,' yet somehow and inexplicably they have often done this in very shallow water. They are, according to the official versions, supposed to have walked miles or many blocks, in the wrong direction, until they reach a remote body of water, and then drowned.

Curiously, some of them have been in towns they have never visited until that night, only to be found in remote ponds that they could never have known even existed, nor the route to take to get to them. Alternately, they appear to have scaled fences or other difficult obstacles to get into remote ponds and then drowned in water that is no deeper than a couple of feet.

Are there any clues which could help explain what has happened to these young men, and why?
Why are many of them found missing one shoe?
Why are their cell phones often found beside the river's edge, again as though purposely placed there?
Why have some of their bodies been 'placed' into positions which are wholly inconsistent with that of a drowning victim?

Someone who drowns will usually be found floating face down in the water. One victim was on his back and had his arms crossed over his body. Another was 'bobbing' up in the water in an upright position. Another was held in place by two small sticks; 'displayed' there waiting to be found.

Why have some of the bodies been found 'half-in and half-out' of the water? Like Henry McCabe, like Mike Knolls.
Why do some of the toxicology reports show drugs that the boys were never known to have taken?
Why have they not fought back or struggled? Very often, they have no injuries whatsoever; indicating that they have not struggled, even though they were drowning. Obviously the very sinister implication here then is that they were either unconscious or dead when they entered the water. Some even have no water at all in their lungs; yet they have apparently "drowned" in the water.

Drowning in water is not a common suicide method, with less than 4% of men choosing this method. In fact, it's especially difficult to commit suicide in shallow water, and furthermore, it would require weighing oneself down to make the body heavier.

The bodies when found, are often not in the state in which they would be expected to be found. Sometimes their deaths are 'inconclusive,' or 'undetermined.' Sometimes the pathologists openly rule that the cause of death will probably never be determined; which is itself highly alarming given that law enforcement then refuse to follow up on the cases and investigate them. They are just said to have simply drowned, *somehow*.

The original retired detectives who investigated over a decade ago, found that in some of these cases, the young men had been held, drugged, mentally tortured, physically tortured, killed, and then taken to the water and placed in it.

Strangely, a common factor is that many times the young men have been seen in the presence of not only unknown young people, but cops and bouncers too. Nothing strange there perhaps; but maybe it's not that clear cut.

Several of the men have even phoned friends to say that 'someone' or 'people' are after them, that they are in fear for their lives and that they 'haven't done anything wrong.' Who is after them? And does this implicate the police, or perhaps people pretending to be the police?

Why are there other stories floating around of possible 'near misses,' in which the young men describe attempts by strangers to lure them outside? Why do some of the parents of the deceased young men talk about the 'unknown' people being at the scene of their disappearance? Of strangers chasing them, and of being terrified for their lives?

Why do many of them make desperate phone calls just moments before something happens to them?

Why are some of them in such a state of terror or horror when they phone their parents or friends?

Why would their cell phones suddenly go dead after they have said something very disturbing?

What are they seeing, in the final moments before their phone is cut off?

Why are they later found in places searched multiple times before?

Why are their bodies 'placed' in strange positions, as though arranged by someone?

Why are many missing one shoe?

Why do few of them have any signs of injury?

What did one boy mean, "Look in the periodic table" before he vanished?

Why is graffiti sometimes found referring to Hydrogen? Hydrogen originates from the Greek word, 'Genes, genetics, and DNA.'

Why does a leading criminologist say, "This is terrorism; they operate as cells." But, it's not terrorism as we usually understand it; it's something very, very different.

How could this have anything to do with the alleged occurrences of 'false flags?' or 'black ops'?

Why did one boy's scent track to an Abbey in an area he had never been to while alive? Why were priests at that Abbey describing an occult drowning ritual on an esoteric forum? This is just the beginning of one possibility...

What does a taunting message posted in a forum referring to a man who is said to be immortal, mean? Are the people who are doing this communicating online? Are cryptic or bragging messages being left that we have overlooked?

Is this all hyperbole and exaggeration? Is it looking for things that simply aren't happening? Or, does a very unusual cabal exist, that no-one would ever have thought of; obsessed with both deliverance and immortality, and the evidence suggests they are more powerful than the illuminati? They believe they cannot be caught. They believe they are above reproach; they believe they are untouchable.

Or, is the simplest answer; drink and misadventure? Vance Holmes, who runs the blog 'Drowning in Coincidence' and who has followed these cases when they were first believed to have started, asks in one of the cases, how the young man would even have been capable of getting to the river in which he was found drowned, given his intoxication. Calling it "too drunk to drown," his says, of 21 year old Lucas Homan, how did he end up dead in the Mississippi river?

"I understand he may have been drinking. I understand he may have stumbled away from his friends unnoticed. I understand that at the water's edge, he may have accidentally fallen in. What I don't understand is how he got to the river in the first place. His blood alcohol was 0.32 %."

Holmes then quotes from a guide, provided by a breath-testing company, citing the symptoms of anyone who has a blood alcohol reading in the range of 0.25-0.40 %. They are as follows; 'Inability to stand or walk, stupor, loss of motor functions, impaired consciousness; sleep or stupor.' "
How then did Lucas get to the river at all?"

The estimated number of cases is now well over 300, according to profilers. The predominant cases are those where young men have been 'kicked out' of bars by bouncers, yet it later turns out, they have invariably been wrongly accused of being drunk or disorderly. Then they are found dead in water, days, weeks, or even months later, usually in areas where searches have occurred multiple times. Some have been drinking and are drunk; many others are not drunk in any way, with no alcohol in their system.

Curiously, there are other cases that are even stranger. How do some of the young men end up extremely drunk to the point of nausea and disorientation, so quickly once inside a bar? Those who have been found to be drunk, are excessively 'drunk;' so much so that it would seem impossible for them to have walked to the remote water where they are found dead weeks or months later.

Many have appeared so disoriented and confused that they have had to leave the Bar or Party they are attending. Some have later been found to have had drugs in their system; drugs their close friends knew they never took. Again, it can easily be dismissed as youth and misadventure; but there have been many cases where disorientation takes place so quickly and so suddenly that the suggestion is their drinks are being tampered with. Moreover, when the men are later found dead in the water, there have been several cases where MDMA or GHB or sedatives have been found in their systems. None of the young men were ever known to have taken these drugs nor were they being prescribed sedatives.

How does a young man appear fine one moment, disoriented and confused the next, then suddenly disappear, and then end up dead in water that is only a couple of feet deep? Why can he not be found for often what amounts to weeks? Why would he go to the most remote body of water, always in the opposite direction to that which he was heading?

Of the ones who were kicked out, very often for reasons which are either spurious and false, or later flatly denied, why are these boys purposely 'separated' from their friends; isolated and made vulnerable, often left outside without their wallets or coats, in winter, and then later found in bodies of water? In almost every case, why have even those who have had nothing to drink, walked in the exact opposite direction to that which they told their friends they were heading, back to their home?

How do they then end up dead in water, often having apparently climbed over high fences and 'jumped' into ponds or retention tanks, just a few inches deep, and 'forgotten how to swim?' How do very fit wrestlers, sportsmen, and most notably, boys on swim teams, end up dead in shallow water, only inches deep, having suddenly become unable to swim?

Why have they then often made very disturbing phone calls after they disappear? Why are several of them screaming down the phone before it goes dead? What are they seeing? Who or what is there, with them? Who is taking them? And why? And where are the missing ones who are never found?

Chapter 2:
Current Day - Cryptic Clues

Returning to the current case of missing Harvard student Zachary Marr, who disappeared in Boston on the night of the 13th of February, 2016, the News has gone quiet now. His family are understandably frantic with worry. Last week, the police said; "It appears the surveillance images capture him entering the water."

They have not, and probably will not be releasing this surveillance footage to the general public, and since they have searched the water again without finding him, there has been no more news coverage.

The day the police released this statement they searched the water thoroughly with divers, but they did not find him. What does not make any sense is the reason why he would even consider entering the water; ice cold water, late at night, when he had only stepped outside the Pub to have smoke a cigarette? The notion that he then decided to either go for a swim, mid-winter, or drown himself, is an abnormal and nonsensical idea.

His family and his friends at this point in time have expressed no details on him ever being suicidal. There is simply nothing that would suggest that he voluntarily and willingly took himself down to the water and jumped in, fully clothed, in the middle of winter; and as is apparent from studying the hundreds of cases that came before his, this is a commonality of shocking recurrence.

One hopes he is not going to become another one to add to the statistics; one hopes he will soon be found and there will be a perfectly reasonable and logical explanation as to how and why he disappeared; that he decided to take off for a holiday somewhere on his own, to take some time out, or he met a girl and they ran off together; anything other than that he will be found dead in the water.

The thing is, it has happened at the right time of year for this; the months in which this happens is not in the summer months; it's the winter months. It ranges from September to April, the coldest months. It doesn't happen in the months most expected, which in itself highlights just how strange these cases are.

At this point, the statements from the police do not indicate anything other than that he voluntarily walked to the water, and got in. This 'theory,' if law enforcement were to consider the vast number of young men who have died exactly this way over the last few months, and years, is a theory that cries out to be investigated from different angles. 'Suicide' or 'accidents' do not do the young men and their families' justice in any way. Something very unusual is happening to them, as this book will attempt to illustrate.

For Harvard man Zachary, he was visiting Boston and was on a night out with his cousins, on February 13th, in the Bell in Hand Pub. He was celebrating his birthday; something that many of the victim's are doing when they disappear.

A commonality again in these cases appears to be that many of the disappearances and drownings occur either on birthdays or holidays, such as Henry McCabe's Labor Day, Chris Jenkins's Halloween, Brian Shaffer's Spring Break, Thomas Hecht's St Patrick's day.

How this ties in could be simply coincidence; or it could mean something far more sinister. It could mean that the young men are being targeted and tracked prior to their disappearances, an idea which will be further elaborated on as this book progresses.

Zachary stepped outside to have a smoke, and he can be seen on surveillance footage, smoking, and pacing a little as he does so; a habit that many smokers have and certainly there is nothing whatsoever in this footage to suggest he is in any way upset or disturbed or unhappy about anything. He certainly does not look suicidal nor does he look intoxicated; he just looks like a handsome young man having a cigarette; and the perfect specimen for those who are doing the targeting. It is almost always handsome, young, white males. Sometimes it is other ethnic groups, but not very often.

His cousins later said that when he tried to go back into the Pub, he was refused re-entry. The Pub issued a statement, after it was announced in the News that he had gone missing. They disputed this version, making a public statement saying, "We have provided video to the police and it showed Zachary leaving at 1:20 am. The video clearly shows that he did not try to re-enter. It does however show several other customers leaving, and re-entering. He would not have been denied access."

According to his relatives however, the young man had sent a text to them, telling them that he was being refused re-entry because it was approaching closing time. This is the most alarming detail; not because the Pub were necessarily doing anything wrong, or in any way responsible for his disappearance; it's just that this has been a recurring theme across many States, and indeed even internationally, in England too. Young men are disappearing not only in remote areas, with few to no witnesses, but they are disappearing from outside Bars in busy areas. They are often last seen on Surveillance footage; then they vanish. Sometimes there have been unknown people nearby; people that have not been identified. Then they are simply 'gone.' Other times, they are last seen in the company of bouncers, or the police.

Are they the police, or are they someone impersonating a police officer? It has even been suggested that these young men are being tracked by the cell phones, and in at least one case, a cell phone blocker was used.

Twenty one days before Zacharry disappeared, the body of Matthew Genovese was found floating in the Hudson River; the same River that Zacharry may also sadly be in. Matthew, 24, was out with work friends in Hoboken, New Jersey. Matthew had last been seen by his friends that night, inside the Pub. He left the Pub at around 10.30 p.m. His friends stated that he was not intoxicated. It was a Saturday night, January 23rd, 2016. He left to go home; a walk he knew very well and one that should have taken him 10 minutes.

The following Monday, when he didn't arrive at work, his work called his family to see why he was absent. It was his family who then reported him missing, being unable to get hold of him, and having determined that no-one had seen or heard from him since Saturday night.

When he left the Pub it had been snowing heavily, but his walk was not too far. His friends who had been at the bar with him said they did not think he was drunk when he left. The next day, on Tuesday, a detective searching by the Pier and river, found his wallet with his credit cards and cash still inside, as well as his keys, beside Pier A in Hoboken. If his money was all still lying there, then that would surely seem to suggest that he was not the victim of a robbery; but why would he have gone down to the river at all? Particularly in such bad weather, when it was snowing and freezing cold.

He was not wearing a thick warm coat, and surely anyone would have chosen to go straight home rather than head to the water? It seemed that he must have headed East after leaving the Pub, rather than West; the direction in which his apartment lay.

With his wallet being found at the site in which he was thought to have gone into the water, it was almost as though *someone* had left it there, on purpose; wanting it to be found. It doesn't seem reasonable to suggest that Matthew would have taken his wallet and keys out, placed them on the ground, then jumped into the water. It was a freezing cold night. It didn't make any sense.

It also didn't make any sense that he got hopelessly lost, totally disoriented, in an area he knew very well, and walked in a completely different direction to that of his apartment, and didn't stop until he reached water and then jumped in. When his body was recovered from the water, the police said there was no obvious trauma on his body. Toxicology results are pending.

An investigator not related to the official investigation contacted me recently to show me some photographs of what he says were found near the scene; A drawing of two eyes and a mouth; Graffiti found at Pier 1, at the site where his body was recovered, with the word;

"H3yme."

Is this a sickening taunt?

H3yme; 'yme,' "Why me?"
Or is it just a simple graffiti tag, one that doesn't have to make sense to outside observers, and is totally unrelated to the death of Matthew? Quite possibly.

'Hy3' is in the periodic table. It's Tritium; Hydrogen3. One of its identifiers is 'SMILE.' (Simplified molecular-input line line-entry system). Of course, when these killings were first publicized, in the Wisconsin area, and New York State, two retired NYPD detectives were tracking the graffiti left at the scenes of the young men who had been found in the water. It was very clear to them that the young men had not gone willingly into the water. It was also very clear to them, that this graffiti was related.

Of course, many have dismissed this graffiti as being irrelevant, and they could be correct, but it could also be a message left in plain site. As for the retired detectives, they would argue that it's easy to dismiss when those dismissing it have not walked the crime scene like they did, with decorated Ret'd Detective Gannon even going so far as funding his own investigations by re-mortgaging his home, so convinced was he of the crimes and so adamant in his desire to stop this from continuing to happen. The most sinister one was found in Iowa. It was a face drawn in red with devil horns. Next to the face was a note that read, "Evil

Happy Smiley Face Man." Again, we can accept or dismiss this as evidence; but this is not all of the potential evidence it seems.

Is this still happening? Are messages still being left, in cryptic ways? Unless the investigators in each drowning death are looking for it, they probably won't come across it. Having spoken with the original profiler on this case, he is of the opinion that without any doubt, messages are still being left, in various forms. He also pointed to the international aspect of these deaths, asking me if I had been following an out-break of drowning deaths in Ireland. When I took a cursory look into them, I found a graffiti smiley face. Just chance and luck? Well, it's just one of the many mysteries involved in these cases.

Of course, this could and quite possibly is an absolute red herring, something that in fact is just a series of random graffiti. In the complexity of these cases, and with the realm of possible suspects being exceptionally wide-ranging, it's easy to hone in on one aspect and run with it, in the full belief that you are onto something big.

It's easy to lose subjectivity in the frantic attempt to solve these deaths and to stop them. As this book will show, nothing here is that simple. The possibilities are a quagmire; they are muddied, and confusing, and they potentially run very deep. The graffiti is just one tiny part of it.

But if we return to the graffiti allegedly left at the scene of Matthew's death; a face and 'H3yme,' it's interesting to note that 'Trituim,' a constituent of H3, is what's currently spilling out of the Fukashima nuclear plant. Tritium was also the isotope used in the H-bomb. H3 however is mostly comprised of H_2O, (water) so, it appears to be an explicit reference to Water; or we could say, to a massive and genocidal incident.

If we take just the water part however; obviously, this is the very thing that the boys are ending up dead in. Is this a mocking message? On the other hand, H3yme is also the name of some twitter users, several in fact; and therefore it's entirely possible that it's also the signature of a graffiti artist, particularly given that the Newspapers there have mentioned the graffiti problem in Hoboken (just like in any other town or city.)

H3 also happens to be the name of a computer game too though; and here we have two overlaps; two cases very similar, but with different endings, as will be explained. The computer game H3 was launched in 2007, as a first person shooter game, played on Xbox. Neo Babson Maximus, a different boy, was a world class player at another first person shooter computer game called, 'Half-Life.' Neo Babson Maximus left a cryptic message for his sister, when he told her, while fleeing through the woods just before he disappeared, "Look under the Periodic Table."

So, we have another boy, who vanished under inexplicable circumstances, whose case also features the Periodic Table of Elements; and a Computer Game. Two separate possibilities mirrored in two of the cases; and more, in fact.

It's interesting to note that communication through these types of Computer Games are almost impossible to monitor; and that is why terrorists use them. Communicating through online gaming enables messages that are sent between cells of terrorists like ISIS, to disappear and leave no trace. They are perfect for illicit conversation and almost impossible to track. Messages dissipate, they are not permanent. Forbes Magazine wrote about this in the after-math of the Paris bombing in 2015. 'Two Call of Duty players could write messages to each other on a wall in a disappearing spray of bullets. It may sound ridiculous, but there are many ways like that which would almost be impossible to track.'

Whistleblower Snowden revealed that the NSA and the CIA embed themselves into online computer games such as World of Warcraft, in an attempt to try and infiltrate virtual terrorist meet-ups. Of course, the ability to find communication from this 'group' who abduct and drown young men would be impossible to track down unless NSA or the FBI were to do the same thing as they do in their attempts to infiltrate terrorists. It would require tapping into an enormous amount of activity; and what would seem a nearly impossible task, unless they knew what or who they were specifically looking for.

However, if we accept domestic terrorism and gang stalking expert, Professor Lee Gilbertson's theory, that whoever is doing this is operating like terrorist cells do, then perhaps this is something that should be looked into.

Then there is the Dark Web, via the Onion Router; where anonymity is virtually, although not always, guaranteed.

Could the killers be liaising openly on the Internet? Or, would they be using such tools as described above, along with, for example, Snap-chat, where text messages disappear after reading?

On the other hand, if people aren't specifically looking for clues and hidden messages online, it's possible they have been leaving them all along. Would they want their messages to be found? Are there many groups who don't want people to take notice of their atrocities? Are there many that don't like to openly brag about what they are doing and getting away with? Don't they usually like to taunt and put it in people's faces? Even higher level operations such as the Secret Societies and illuminati are said to leave messages in plain sight aren't they?

One consideration of course is that a lot of these abductions and deaths occurred in the '80's and '90's, when the internet was still in its infancy and there was no Dark Web. Trying to find if they have left messages is quite probably a completely impossible task, one which would take weeks, months and probably years. It would also require a digital forensics expert. However, maybe even an amateur could attempt to find them. What if they really were leaving messages? Where would they be found?

Perhaps there are messages in this case; that of Neo, the Half-Life gamer, as referenced above. It's a highly strange case, and it started when a terrified and barely coherent call came from Charles Allen Jr as he ran for his life through the woods. Charles had only recently officially changed his name to Neo Babson Maximus. He'd formerly been one of the top gamers in the world, and he'd changed his name, in part, to reflect his infamous online persona. The game he was reported as playing the most was called 'Half-Life,' at which he was no. 1 in the world for some time.

The game revolves around the central character of a Scientist who must fight his way out of a secret underground research facility where Research and Development experiments into teleportation technology have gone disastrously wrong. He was a University of Massachusetts Dartmouth senior, four hours away from Boston, and he was studying psychology.

It was October 11, 2007, when his sister called him to ask him why he had deleted his facebook profile. He replied that he hadn't and then began to become very frightened and frantic. He told his sister that people were after him and he wasn't safe. His sister has said that he sounded confused; that he wasn't making any sense to her.

He told her to go home to their parents because she too was now not safe, and that only their Father could protect her. He said he had sent emails to 'important people;' and that now these same people were after him. He told her to 'Look under the periodic table of elements' for the answer; then he ended the call abruptly.

That was the last time she spoke to him. He called his parents and left what his Father says were "strange messages" on their voicemails. He sounded like he was running at the time, and it would later transpire that he was running in the woods. Then his phone was turned off.

According to his friends at University, he'd been having a normal day at college before he made those calls. None of them knew that Charlie had to take medication for bi-polar disorder, and although he had decided to stop taking his medication a while ago, believing he no longer needed it, despite this however, his behaviour was still totally normal; so much so that his friends were completely shocked when they learned he had a condition at all.

His parents too said that from their interaction with him, they did not spot any signs that his behaviour was in any way about to spiral out of control. They said he had also never suffered any kind of breakdown in the past.

Did he have a psychotic breakdown? That's what most people will probably think, when looking at the case, while others might say that it would be a very strong coincidence that he happened to believe his life was in danger and that people were after him, and then he disappeared because he just happened to be in the wrong place in the woods at the wrong time.

Surely, the chances of that are pretty minimal? A young man goes into the woods running to attempt to evade what he claims are people after him, and then goes missing because of a different reason entirely?

According to his friends, he'd spent the day at college, and played tennis with a friend; a game at which he was said to be taking very seriously, with the intention of hopefully playing professionally. He'd arranged to meet a friend later that evening in the college car park to go to a party. He never showed up.

The next night, he broke into a woman's home and entered the bedroom, believing it was the home of his friend, Mason. When the woman whose home he was in woke up, he apologized politely and then jumped out of the *second floor* window to the ground, and ran off into the woods.

Interestingly, his case is reminiscent of that of Mike Knoll, who also wandered disoriented into a woman's home in November 2002, in another part of the country, after disappearing outside of a bar. Four months later his body was found 'positioned' half-in and half-out of a lake that had been searched and dragged multiple times.

Neo's sneakers and backpack were found in the woods. He is still missing. When the police investigated his computer, they found that everything had been cleaned out of it. His family never believed for one moment that he himself would voluntarily delete everything including his emails from his computer.

Who were the "Important people? he said he had contacted?" What had he said to them, and why would they then be "after him."

Ever since then, thousands of people, both those who knew him and many others online, have tried to unlock the clue in his quote; "look under the periodic table for the answer."

It seemed to be all there was to go on after private investigators and the police failed to find the missing

boy. Like Matthew Genovese's alleged graffiti, 'H3yme,' "why me?" Neo may also have been referring to an element in the Periodic table. One person, Jacob Vaughan, thinks he found the answer;
'The clue in the periodic table may be what they call a Half-Life; I searched the H= Hydrogen Al=Aluminium F=Fluorine (half) Li=Lithium Fe=Iron.'
So, we have another allusion to Elements in the Periodic Table; but, again, like the reference to a Computer Game in Matthew Genovese's case, the computer game Neo was most well known for was called 'Half-Life.' He'd been number 1. in the world at this Game. He'd been widely known in the online world.

Had his abductors been communicating with him through the game? Or was it in some way more related to the Periodic Table?
At the Pier where Matthew Genovese died, the researcher who sent me the "Why me?" graffiti, also sent me a red dot painted at the scene of his entrance into the water, as well as a red dot painted across the street from the Pub that he left that night.

How does this link to a Google keyword search for Matthew Genovese, which led me to a blank website, yet where the words in the search showed up as;
'Mathew Genovese...paint it red.....brb...gotta run to Home Depot.'
(brb= meaning, 'be right back')

Very likely again, we just have a mere coincidence; and in all likelihood, it's probably just another example of looking too hard to try to find clues and links and patterns to try to determine who is doing this; and given that this message was written some time prior to his death in actual fact, this would surely be unrelated? Unless we consider the chilling possibility that the death of this young man was pre-planned.

On the topic of the Periodic Table of Elements once more, another young man, Joseph Smedley, had a picture of the Periodic Table as his front cover picture on Facebook. Perhaps again this is nothing out of the ordinary; he was after all a Biochemistry student.

Perhaps it should be mentioned here however, that Alchemists created the Periodic Table. Alchemists are often described as the first Chemists; they developed an extraordinary language (rather than the chemical symbols we use today) to describe all manner of things, from chemical reactions to philosophical tenets, and Alchemy at its most fundamental is a *principle* or *belief*. It can be the main principles of *a 'religion'* or a *philosophy*. Alchemy is a credo, a dogma, a canon, and a belief. This is important; because it could quite possibly be a vital clue as to the kind of people behind this. This could quite possibly, as will later be discussed, refer to something which, as its motivation, could lie in the realms of the darkest underworld yet be in the search of the highest 'Divine Source;' a search for 'transcendence of the soul,' a search for salvation through 'illumination.' For salvation through dark alchemy. The context of their alchemy? ... It's murder.

This student at Indiana University, Joseph Smedly, also posted on his twitter page in October 2015,
"If I'm found dead....it wasn't suicide. And I don't want peaceful protest." He then tweeted, "Perhaps I have said too much."

Why would he write this? He also sent a text to his sister telling her he was leaving the country. It didn't make any sense, especially as he'd been planning activities with his friends at college over the next few days. Then he just simply vanished.

Whatever was troubling him, whatever was going on, he kept it to himself. His message to his sister reads, "Not telling you is keeping you safe and protected."

When Neo Babson Maximus spoke to his sister, he told her she must get home to their parents fast; that only their father could protect her. He had "sent emails to important people; and now they are after me."

Joseph Smedly also appeared to have people after him. He was reported missing on Monday 28th September. He had last been seen at around 11.30 p.m. the Sunday night before this. He was found dead in Griffy Lake, near to his campus, on October 2nd. His death was ruled suicide on December 5th, 2015, by the

Monroe Country coroner. A fisherman had come across his body. No foul play was suspected.

However, his sister is not satisfied with the official ruling by any means. Vivian writes, "How does one drown themselves in 3 feet of water; tell me? My brother did not commit suicide."

Again, this is a very common theme; young men drowning in just a few inches of water. It does not make any sense at all.

His sister set up a *Justice for Joseph* page, and requested a second autopsy. Since this time, she has been posting disconcerting circumstances that would appear to shed serious doubt on the official ruling.
"I believe it's time for you to know some facts," she says. From reading the report of the Coroner, she discovered that in fact his body had a backpack strapped to his chest, and it was full of rocks. His cell phone was never found, she says, and a 'note' left in his dorms saying 'Goodbye,' she also queries. She says it does not seem to be in her brother's handwriting.

Although her brother had told her he was leaving the country, she thought he had to be joking around. She didn't think he really was; after all, it would have been completely uncharacteristic of him to do something like that. In fact, she also didn't take it seriously because he didn't even have a passport.

What she does consider now however is the possibility that someone else sent her that text; just as she thinks someone else wrote the note. It was signed with his surname only; something she said he never did.

Even weirder, is a reply tweet from his mother; but his Mother didn't have a twitter account, and the account was created that same day. His sister feels this was created to back up his story of going away.

On the other hand, he had to have been concerned by something; or why would he write, "If I'm found dead...it wasn't suicide."

Like Neo Babson Maximus, who disappeared after running through the woods; Joseph Smedly also clearly believed someone was after him. Are these young men being contacted directly through online games they play? In other words, are other 'gamers' or those disguising themselves as 'gamers,' contacting the boys while they are playing, talking to them, in some way slowly forging a trusting 'friendship,' or, even indoctrinating them, brain-washing them in some way, for as yet, an unknown but deadly reason? What is happening in the days prior to the boys disappearing?

Interestingly, 'Joseph Smedley' (a different person to the one who was found drowned) aka 'Smed' aka 'Variety Jones' was the name of one of the people said to have been behind creating the architecture and funding for 'Silk Road;' the Dark Web market for buying and selling *anything* from illegal guns and drugs, to murder for hire. Again, a coincidence here however, although as will later be discussed, there are many people who believe that these young men are deliberately 'picked' according to their names, and that their names and the places at which they are found make patterns and even spell out by words such as 'COP' and 'COLD' for example.

Take this example; In Duluth, New York State, in 2004, two boys disappeared in quick succession. On October 10th, Grant Geiselhart is found dead. That same day Nathan Williams, whose nickname was "Fish," was scheduled to return from his fishing trip in the same area. Later he too is found dead.
Nearby, these words are allegedly found close to Grant Geiselhart's place of death;
'Flow on with the Fishes. GOD Grants Pure Wishes,'
Both of the boy's names appear to some extent within this message.
On the other hand, what can potentially be made of Neo's statement about the Periodic Table, and of the H20 Element left at Matthew Genovese's site?

Taking the keywords of 'Neo Babson Maximus' and 'H2O,' search results on the Internet included a Japanese website. It appeared to be a forum. The messages in this forum appeared to be spam; and yet all three of his names (and they're very unusual names) appeared, alongside 'H20,' and other words that appeared to be talking about fixing a shower; an obviously water-related subject; even perhaps a possible method of drowning the victims?

But surely it's just simply talking about fixing a shower?! And it's just an innocent coincidence that his names were there too? Or, could it in any way have been describing the method of killing these young men; by drowning them in the shower?
Blogs are notoriously unmoderated, as are many forums, particularly older ones; and that is why 'groups' use them to communicate. Could these killers be communicating through unmoderated forums and blogs?

Why would they do this? Because they want it on display; or, because they want to communicate without the fear of being tracked or their phone being tapped, and because some of the killings occurred before the Dark Web.
In order to know if these were real clues or messages of course, a cyber forensic analyst or a coder in the NSA is needed. Until then, this is just my own amateur attempt and I am most likely very wrong. In order to prove this particular theory, it would take both an expert, and a significant amount of time; after all, there are at least 300 similar cases. But perhaps it does show

the importance of thinking laterally when approaching this phenomenon if nothing else.

That message was written 10 years ago, in 2006, a time when the killings were multiple; but before Snapchat and the development of software which enabled messages to disappear once written. It was written a few months prior to Neo's potential death; indicating that if it really was some kind of message, or taunt, it was *pre-planned*. *Indicating that he was targeted and specifically chosen beforehand.*

It's easy to get carried away and see patterns, clues, connections, and possible answers when trying to investigate this phenomenon; a phenomenon which as yet remains wholly unsolved. I'm not the first; hundreds if not thousands of people have attempted to solve it, 'armchair' sleuths who are in fact not amateurs in terms of their potential theories and their analysis of such theories, which have ranged from word association clues found in ancient texts, works of poetry and literature, and other clues found by linking it to the Son of Sam murders, the Mansons, even the unknown killer of JonBenet Ramsey, as well as other such sinister organizations and killers. For many, these cases too have become an obsession.

So, continuing on in my search for clues within the Periodic Table, as just one of the possible answers to this mystery, H20 itself is not in the periodic table; however; another keyword search result on the internet led to this; and this one had not only his name, and H2O, (water) but also the words, 'Half-Life.'

I didn't use the keywords 'Half-Life,' and yet it came up with his full and unusual name and H20.

This message again appeared to look like spam, yet it had his full name in it, as well as 'Half life *multi-player*,' 'H20,' and the abbreviation for bulk Hydrogen, 'bhy.'

Hydrogen is in the periodic table; and it originated from the ancient Greek words 'hydro' and 'genes;' literally meaning genes/genetics and DNA. Whether this is a message or not, it does make one wonder if there is any possibility that these young men are being taken for some kind of genetic or DNA experimentation purposes? The young men are usually Caucasian and of European ancestry.

The same message also had the letters, 'tfgvak'

Merely spam? Well, interestingly, 'tfg' also refers to Genes again; The Protein 'TFG' is a protein that in humans, is encoded by the 'TFG' gene. Among its pathways is the disease Cancer, hereditary motor neurone disease and spastic paraplegia.

How is this relevant; it very probably isn't and it's probably reading too much into things. Yet, interestingly, before Joseph Smedley disappeared, he'd posted an article on twitter concerning 'The Reprogramming of DNA is observed in human cells for the first time.'

Another web search for Joseph Smedley led to a site called "brine.esy.es" Does this sound like "brine e syes" which could mean "Briny Seas?"
'Briny' meaning salt sea water.
Probably nothing relevant again; just coincidence. Do these series of deaths just mentioned really tie in to the Periodic Table? Or Genes? If so, what on earth could be the connection?

As already said, Alchemists were the ones who created the Periodic Table. Alchemists were called 'the first Chemists;' because they developed a language (rather than the chemical symbols we use today) to describe philosophical tenets, and Alchemy at its most fundamental is a *principle* or *belief or religion.*

This is very important; as we will later discover. Alchemy encompassed physics, medicine, astrology, mysticism and spiritualism. The aims of the Alchemists was to find the Stone of Knowledge; the 'Philosopher's Stone;' but not in a literal meaning, more in a symbolic meaning, in searching for the elixir of *Immortality*, of Eternal life, of Perfected Man as a Divine Living God. Esoterically and hieroglyphically, alchemy refers to the mystery of the Primordial, or 'First Matter' from which we and everything else came. More on this will be covered later, but as some experts in this field have pointed out to me; these deaths may very well be the work of arcane alchemical rites, rituals, and sacrifice, which go back centuries.

If we take the name of another possible victim, Ewan Curbeam, one whom the authorities said happened to fall in the water and drown, but others would disagree; a keyword search again on the internet took me to another Japanese forum, again.

Evan had a Master's Degree from George Washington University in systems engineering. He was found in the Inner Harbor in Baltimore, Maryland, just after Thanksgiving in 2013. As with Neo, who was undoubtedly exceptionally bright, Evan was also full of promise. He'd been awarded 'Airman of Year' for his outstanding performance and was a poster boy for a National Guard recruiting campaign.

This keyword search coincidentally led to an online games and sports discussion board, where one of the messages, again which appeared as though spam, and perhaps it was just that, but it had links at the end of the message. I clicked on them. It took me to a Japanese forum, again. It's an article regarding water piping robberies; *water* again. Surely just a coincidence and an overactive imagination? Trying to make connections where none can be found? What this link said, was something that is utterly disturbing. Among the message are the sentences;
"He has video cameras,"
"They also need to have scenario."
And; the complete sentence,

"Comes to an end once you've got a trip originating from a friend near to the College."

These were complete sentences, spread out amid other sentences. Like its a sick game; like 'cells' are being sent out to complete this on their own, according to the 'rules' of how its done, and it ends when they've met up with their 'contact' and are on their way out of town, after the act is completed? After another victim is dead in the water?

Whether these are real clues or not, certainly it has to be more than one person involved, to be able to successfully snatch up a young man, take him away, and return him at a later period in time, dead.

Chapter 3:
The Beginning

The scenarios just presented in the different messages, are just a couple of the many possibilities behind this phenomenon, possibilities which will be presented in depth as this book continues; and it's a phenomenon which some Profilers I have been liaising with claim encompasses more than 300 deaths over many years and is in operation internationally; yet the victim type is almost always the same. Young, handsome, usually Caucasian, outstanding sportsmen, outdoorsmen, and top scholars. Usually they are still in college at the time of their deaths. Usually they happen in the months between September and April. Again, surely this is not what it looks like, surely this is just accidents? Surely this cannot be organized?

While some of the 'drowning' deaths are slow, silent, and hidden operations; a young man disappears while walking home alone in a rural area, with no witnesses and no tracks or trail to determine where he has gone or how; others disappear more publicly. Are there any hints in the more public ones, about who could be doing this? About other people being involved?

Looking again at the more current 'drowning' deaths presented at the beginning of the book, Matthew Genovese, who was found in the Hudson River on

January 23rd, 2016. He isn't the only one to have been found drowned in that river there in recent months. On November 14th 2015, 23 year old Anthony Urena left a nightclub in New York City around 5 a.m. He'd called a cab but for some reason when it came, he decided not to take it. Instead, he walked across to a late night food service stand, to get something to eat, then he wandered away.

As he walked, he was unsteady on his feet and was seen wavering from side to side. On surveillance camera he appears intoxicated, but there's also the strange sighting of a car which comes down the road. It's coming the wrong way down a one way street. It turns round, doubles back and then Anthony disappears from view of the camera.

The police say he must have fallen in the river and drowned. They say that he fell into the Harlem River at some point after he was last seen, and that his body was then swept to the Hudson River.

He wasn't found for more than a month. His uncle, Ray Serrano, said that doesn't make any sense at all. He went to the spot where police said his nephew had fallen in. The water at that spot was below knee deep. How do you drown when the water is just inches deep?

This bears similarity to when Patrick O'Neil disappeared in New York City. Witnesses saw a car double parked as he exited the Bar he'd been drinking in. He appeared very drunk; so much so that he was bending over and uncoordinated. He was clearly feeling nauseous. He attempted to walk off down the street and the double parked car began to move beside him. Patrick stopped as though he was about to be sick, stumbled and fell over. The car beside him stopped.

When Patrick managed to recover and pick himself back up, the car began to follow him again. He was found more than forty days later, dead in the river. That was now nearly 20 years ago. That is how long this has quite possibly been going on for; and it shows no signs of stopping. Like Matt Genovese, Anthony Urena, and the missing Zacharry Marr, David Dreher, a 23 year old man, also went missing after leaving a NYC bar, and was also found in the Hudson River in May 2015.

Again, by the Hudson River, in Boston, on February 8, 2014, graduate Eric Munsell was out celebrating his birthday. It should be noted here, that a large number of these similar incidents do appear to occur while the young men are out celebrating their birthdays, or alternately, celebrating public holidays such as Halloween, and New Year's Eve. Quite possibly this is only a coincidence, and of course, other men have disappeared in the same way on regular nights out; but it does raise the question of whether the young men are perhaps being selected or targeted by people who find out their birth dates.

Eric was in a bar with friends when he was thrown out by a bouncer because, according to his Mother, he had tripped on his way to the bathroom inside the bar, at around 11.30 pm. Ten or so minutes passed before his friends realised he had been thrown out. The bouncers refused to allow her son to have his coat, which had been left inside the bar when he was thrown out. The temperature was below freezing.

Approximately 30 minutes later, his phone was used. At that time, he was headed toward the harbour; a completely different direction to where his apartment was situated.

Later, his parents would sue the Bar for wrongful death; for their part in not providing a duty of care to their son. The law suit claimed that the young man was given no assistance by staff at the bar, despite his impaired state. He was given no help despite being in a vulnerable position due to this intoxication, the suit claims.

What's interesting here of course is that he was "very intoxicated" inside the bar. Now, that again is a commonality among victims. Logically, of course it can be said that he ended up dying because of this intoxication; on the other hand, when this extreme intoxication is a feature of so many of the same type of disappearances and drownings, it does raise a question about how they managed to get so completely intoxicated. It can also be said that friends who have been with the victims, are often very surprised that their friend is that intoxicated.

Of course, someone intoxicated can easily fall victim to misadventure, through lack of reasoning on their part; but what is strange in so many of these cases is that the deaths of these young men occur usually quite some distance from the bars, and always in water.

Aren't they just as likely to walk into the path of a car? Or onto railway tracks, if in the vicinity? Or stumble over and fatally hit their heads on the sidewalk? And so on... Why is it always water? And why do the young men walk toward it, for long distances, completely out of the direction in which they would ordinarily walk? Why does drinking lead to drowning when the water is not beside the bar?

In the lawsuit filed by his parents, his friends state that they observed him appearing to be "un-coordinated, staggering while walking, and intoxicated" when he was on the dance floor of the Bar. The Bar say that he was approached after bumping into other patrons inside the Bar, and subsequently ejected.

The bouncer then stood at the exit and watched as he stumbled off toward the street, "weaving unsteadily on his feet." Other witnesses reported seeing him stumbling and falling into snowbanks. CCTV corroborates their reports.

If he was observed walking falteringly back toward the direction in which his home lay, weaving across the street as he did so, and with his arms crossed over his chest to try to warm himself up, how then did he get to the water?

Also, according to the law suit, he was observed by one witness who said that he had been attempting, unsuccessfully, to get into a residence on the North End area, which was located in the correct direction for his apartment.

It would appear then, that he was truly quite intoxicated, but why would he then head down to the water? If he had been stumbling and falling, how did he even make it back down to the waterfront?

In a very bizarre 'coincidence,' at the same time as police detective Thomas Leahy was searching for this missing young man, in the area of the Long Wharf, he spotted a man in the river struggling to pull himself out of it. The man was trying to climb up the stone wall that bordered the water, and the detective rushed to help him out of the water.

The detective described the man as a non-English speaker, and said that he was not able to explain how he had landed up in the water. Had this other man just had a very near miss himself? If he was a non-English speaker, perhaps he was in the country illegally and afraid of talking too much because he might be arrested. Perhaps something happened to him that would have been very useful to know.

Eric's body was discovered in the same spot in the water; but two months later. A passer-by had seen his "non-viable" body floating in the water.

The question is; why did it take so long for his body to surface in the water? If he had gone in the water on the night of his disappearance, he would surely have been seen long before two months had passed. It's true that a body can become caught on weeds or other natural obstacles in the water, but not every time.

Had he been in the water all that time; or had he been elsewhere? His initial autopsy said that there were "no signs of foul play."

Was the case of this young man purely down to excessive intoxication? Perhaps that is indeed the answer; but on the other hand, why did his body not surface for nearly two months if he had gone to the river and drowned that night?

Retired Det. Kevin Gannon, interviewed in February 2016 by Sybille Marcellus of *Chasing News*, has for a long time been perplexed about the number of young men mysteriously drowning, and not just in this particular part of the United States. With reference to the older drowning cases in particular, of which he identified at least 100 as being the same 'modus operandi', he said, "Is this kid one of those cases; I would not be able to say without looking at the autopsy and toxicology reports. These are dump jobs. This is scientifically proven through forensics; a lot of these young men have been at bars, they have been abducted, even held for a period of time, murdered on land, and they weren't drowned; they're not drowning. Most of these cases are what we call 'dump jobs, 'meaning they're murdered and dumped into these bodies of water."

The young men, over at least a period of the last decade or so, are being found dead in water. The police are invariably ruling these deaths as suicides or, more commonly, 'accidental drownings.' For that reason, the police investigation is minimal to say the least.

When Ret'd Detective Gannon and Detective Anthony Duarte began their own private investigation into these deaths, they initially found that at least 40 young student males had lost their lives in the most sinister of ways.
Some of the boys had been abducted, held for extended periods of time, and according to them, "mentally tortured, sometimes physically."
Who would be doing this? And why?

The cases they looked into spanned many States, and sometimes two college boys disappeared in different States, on the same night. Then later they turned up dead in the water, with no water in their lungs.

Of course, the first thing that comes to mind is: Serial Killer, but it's not that easy. A Serial Killer can't cover the vast ground between the two disappearances that occur on the same night. A pair of Serial Killers? Well, it probably requires more than one 'killer' at each site to man-handle their victim and successfully abduct them.

Often, the victims are last seen in the company of strangers; sometimes young women, which in itself would not suggest anything sinister; after all, they are young men, out having a drink and a good time in Bars; but sometimes they have been seen last in the company of older couples, large groups of unidentified young people, and other times, in the company of men not known to them or the friends they have gone to the Bars with.

The modus operandi of whomever is doing this, appears to be to ensure that their 'target' is purposely separated and isolated; made vulnerable enough to ensure that their 'snatch' is easy, swift, and successful.

Why have some of their bodies 'placed' into positions which are wholly inconsistent with that of a drowning victim? Why have some of the bodies been found 'half-in and half-out' of the water? Like Henry McCabe, like Mike Nolls.

Why very often do they have no injuries whatsoever; indicating that they have not struggled, even though they were drowning? Obviously, the very sinister implication here then is that they were either unconscious or dead when they entered the water. Some even have no water at all in their lungs; yet they have apparently "drowned" in the water.

Strangely, a common factor is that many times the young men have been seen in the presence of not only unknown young people, but cops and bouncers too. Nothing strange there perhaps; but maybe it's not that clear cut.

This next case, for example, offers the very real possibility that the young men are being unwittingly targeted and drugged; In Tupper Lake, Northern New York State, Colin Ellis had returned on spring break from his pre-med course at Brockport State University. He'd gone to a party to see some of his old school friends. Later, his brother would make a memorial video about Colin. In it, he says, "Colin went to a party one night....then no-one heard from him, no-one really saw him; they just found his I.D. and personal belongings on the road, and that was the last of him."

Four hundred local people would turn up to help look for him. The whole community came together. He was said to have been the nicest, kindest soul anyone could wish to meet. He was very handsome, and everyone knew him for his gorgeous smile. He was very bright, always ready to joke, but an intelligent debater. He was, according to those who knew him, one of the most genuine young men you could meet. He was very popular, and no-one had a bad word to say about him. He was a positive influence on everyone who knew him, and he had a very promising future.

At around 1.45 a.m. on the morning of March 11, 2012, a motorist saw a young man walking along a remote stretch of Route 3 in the Adirondack forest. This motorist was concerned by the appearance of the young man as he reached alongside him, because as he had been driving toward him, the young man had been walking with no coat on, close to the white line of the road, and "flailing his arms."

The motorist, Mr Rosentreter, a local resident and the editor of the local newspaper *The Lake Placid News*, thought at first that the young man was attempting to hitch-hike, but something about the way his arms were flailing around also made him think this was not the case. He was concerned, but not knowing the boy personally and with his elderly mother in the passenger seat, he was also cautious about stopping and asking the young man if he was ok. Instead, he drove to the nearest police station only a couple of miles away and reported what he had seen.

Within ten minutes, the police arrived at the spot where the young man had been seen and searched the stretch of road. He was no longer there. He'd been walking in the direction away from the party, and away from his home.

Later, a former schoolmate came forward to report that he'd seen his friend walking along the road and had pulled over to offer him a ride home. He said that Colin declined his offer, telling him he was waiting for a ride from a friend.

When one of his siblings, Lyndon, was later asked why they thought their brother had been walking in the opposite direction to his home, he said, "No-one knows. That's the million dollar question."

The following Monday, during a massive search mission, authorities came across his driver's I.D. together with one of his sneakers, lying on the roadside, in the same area in which he had disappeared. This was initially reported in the Newspapers; by *WHEC* Rochester News, however, after this initial newspaper report, it appears that the story about the missing shoe was for some reason redacted in later editions.

Later reports worded it as, "One of the first parties to go out Monday found a piece of Colin's personal effects on the edge of the south side of the road, west of the intersection of Route 3 and Setting Pole Dam Road, where their search began. Police say the search crew found two of his belongings, but did not go into detail."

This perhaps is a vital clue, if indeed it is accurate. One shoe being left behind, sometimes both shoes, is a commonality among the cases in which young college men have vanished. The meaning behind this is not easily apparent, other than the obvious; that it means as a "message" in the form of a taunt.

Also, given that his I.D. was on the road, did someone ask him for I.D. when he was walking along that road? What kind of people would request I.D.?...

Or, was he involved in a desperate struggle which resulted in it falling out? It could even be asked, was he asked his name and his I.D. checked to make sure they had got the right *one*? In other words, had it been pre-planned and he specifically targeted?

Continued searches involved Forest Rangers, helicopter crews, State Troopers, Northern Search and Rescue Adirondacks Special Operations Response Team members, Fire Department crews, and hundreds of volunteers. It was a "type 3" search, where searchers are positioned just a few feet apart. The local news wrote that the search was "so tight that volunteers who were smokers were told they should light up before they left; because there wouldn't be any time to stop for a smoke once the search commenced."

At some point into the searches, focus shifted from the roads and the woods to the waterways, with each body of water being thoroughly searched. Police said they had looked along the river banks and in the water. The police Captain at the time was confident they had been over the area "with a fine tooth comb."

"Could we have missed him? I don't think it's likely," said Captain Tibbits.

The State police at the time looked into reports that the missing young man had walked away from the party after there had been an argument, but the police have not released details of any investigation into this suggestion. At the time, there was no evidence along the road of any kind neither of altercation nor of a car accident. Nor were there any signs that the young man had tried to walk across a frozen river in the area.

Some crime reporters have tried to suggest that he could have become prey to the serial killer Israel Keyes, who lived not far from the location. However, the F.B.I. is certain that Keyes was using the stolen ATM card of his latest victim in Texas at the time of this young man's disappearance. Colin's phone had last been used about fifteen minutes prior to the sighting of him flailing his arms. His phone has not been found.

His Father says, "He was in an area he knew like the back of his hand." He'd been born and raised there; he couldn't get lost. However, as has been the case in so many of these disappearances, if this case is indeed tied to the others, again he was walking in the opposite direction to that which anyone would have expected him to be walking.

The night that he left for the party, his family all said that he had not acted any different or said anything out of the ordinary. Nothing had seemed strange or odd. He'd been looking forward to catching up with his old friends and they said that he'd been joking around before he left home, talking about how all his friends at college had bought an abs machine so they could get the same shape he had; he was muscular, fit, and certainly in shape. He was over six feet tall. He was not an 'easy target;' and yet against someone with a gun, he would not have had much chance.
Why was he flailing his arms around? What had happened to him to make him do that?

Of course, in some of the cases, the young men have been found to have had drugs in their system; drugs they were never known to have taken before, and when the original investigators were looking into this privately a decade ago, they were certain that many of those young men had been drugged.

What had happened between approximately 1.30 a.m., when a friend of his, Austin Toohey, says he spotted Colin walking home not far from the party, and he'd stopped to offer him a ride, and shortly after, when Austin had returned along that same stretch of road, having dropped his cousin home?
The local news editor, Mr Rosentreter, spotted him not many minutes after this. "He was almost in the road.

He seemed to be acting a little odd. That warranted some concern on my part," he says.

As to what has happened to this young man, his brother has said, "I've dreamed of my brother being dead, kidnapped by the CIA for training, and anything else you could imagine."

Tragically, now four years on, he has still not been found.

What happened to this next young man?
Austin Hudson-Lapore loved numbers, equations, and formulas. Described by his mother as having "a fierce intellect," he was studying biochemistry at Chicago University and wanted to do a doctorate. From that description, he doesn't sound like a young man who was into heavy partying and hard drinking, as has been the accusation most commonly used when these young men are found in rivers.

Austin left his off-campus apartment on the evening of Wednesday June 12, 2013, and simply disappeared. He was not seen again, apart *from perhaps one man, who was driving along* Chicago's South Loop section when he saw someone, who he believes, strongly resembled the young man. By this stage he had been missing for *several days*. Which means, he had been held somewhere quite possibly, and drugged.

On the day he went missing, he'd sat his final exam and had been relaxing with his roommates. He'd been on the internet just before he left, and when he went out, he didn't take his wallet or phone. He never returned. Days later, the driver came forward to say that he almost ran a young man over, a man who appeared to look very much like Austin. He said the young man was crossing the road against the traffic lights. The police reported this to the Media, during the search for Austin. "The driver said the young man was *stumbling* and *unresponsive* and *appeared disoriented* when he called out to ask if anything was wrong."

On June 19, his body was recovered from Lake Michigan. It has since been suggested that he'd gone out to chase the storm that was brewing and to watch the water as it came. It's been called a tragic accident. What has not been determined however, is, if it was the same young man that the driver saw, who he himself believed it was and had called the police to tell them about, why was it that he was "stumbling, unresponsive, and disoriented," having not been in a Bar and having had no alcohol? Also, where had he been in the days he had been missing?

On February 6th, 2016, the body of Ohio Wesleyan University freshman Luke Gabbert was found in a creek in Delaware. No-one knows how he ended up in the water. Ohio Weslyan News Journal *The Transcript* writes, "A crescent moon had risen in the sky when

Luke and a friend wandered back from Clancey's Pub. Only one would make it back to campus."

Luke was found dead in a muddy stream flowing near the college campus. His autopsy report says there was no obvious cause of death and his body showed no visible signs of trauma. Toxicology results will take up to 2 months. *The Transcript* says they carried out their own investigation into the timeline of events surrounding his death. The night before, the freshman had made his pledge to the Phi Kappa Psi (Phi Psi) Fraternity. On his last night alive, the following night, he had been in the Pub, where according to another new pledge of the fraternity, who was with him, he had been asked to leave after being sick inside the Pub. They left together, but on seeing a police car nearby, they apparently split up and went separate ways, for some reason worried about the police pulling them over for questioning. That was the last time anyone allegedly saw him alive.

It has to be said that some looking into these deaths think that perhaps there is fraternity involvement in them. Some people have even said that this goes back years, referring to the name of a man with the surname Smiley; said to be an older member of one of the Fraternities and of course, tying it in to the alleged 'Smiley faces' left at some scenes. Of course, this is just someone's opinion and certainly it has no validity in terms of saying that this man has anything to do with it. What it does do however, is to serve as another example of how far people will go to try to find the answer to what is happening.

Rocky Euenguino, says, "All of the victims are college age men. Fraternities are set up in a hierarchy, with several chapters ran by one head chapter; that way orders or quotas can be issued, to be carried out on specific dates and times, nationally and internationally. Each chapter has a quota. Again don't take my word for it, but keep in mind that 40% of all MK ultra research Psyop programs were delegated to college fraternities and it's an active program, still going strong today."

On February 20th, 2016, 23 year old James Dyer's body was found in the water near Dimrillo's Marina, at Commercial Street, Portland. It was 51 days after he disappeared while out celebrating New Year's Eve. The water in which he was found was situated beside the street he was last seen on.

Bodies surface after ten days; why had he not been seen before this? Had he been in the water all that time, or not? The Coast Guard had constantly been out on the water looking for him. His autopsy is still pending at the time of writing.

In the two months that he was missing, the water had been repeatedly searched with ultra-sophisticated sonar equipment. Volunteer searchers had also repeatedly looked for the missing man. An avid sailor and swimmer, as well as outdoorsman, James had last been seen as he left Pearl nightclub with two friends, in the early hours of New Year's Day. No person's of interest or suspects have been revealed at present time.

The police said that they had reviewed all available footage from security cameras dotted around the area, but found no clues in them. Police spokesman Chris Hardiman expressed his perplexity,
"He is with a group of friends, and then - he's missing! We've heard nothing of him."

His mother Amy, having spoken with his friends, has managed to piece together what she can before he vanished. His friends told her that her son suddenly disappeared outside the Club, on New Year's Eve, when the streets were quite busy. After that, her son's phone appeared to have gone dead, she says, and so his friends began shouting and calling out for him when they realised they had lost him. Then they went to where they had parked their car, and waited for him there; but he never turned up. Sadly, his Mother wasn't told by them that her son had not joined them at the car, and she wasn't aware that he'd vanished until the following evening.

She says it was completely out of character for her son not to show up anywhere. He was always dependable and always contacted her and turned up on time for his job as an Operations Manager on nights shifts at a supermarket. When he didn't arrive for his shift, she became even more concerned. The district he was last seen in, as well as the water, was repeatedly searched and canvassed, over the next fifty days.

If his body had been there in that water all that time, in that busy Harbor, wouldn't it have been seen before 50 days had passed?

Chapter 4: Personal Interest

There are so many more cases; some that have been mentioned in my previous book series, 'In the Woods;' written a couple of years ago, and they're still happening. They are not stopping; they are growing ever more.

I'm not the first to look into these deaths; it began over a decade ago when decorated retired NYPD Detectives Kevin Gannon and Anthony Duarte discovered that at least 40 drowning deaths of young college-aged men were connected. Detective Gannon and Professor Lee Gilbertson of St Cloud University, a specialist in Gang Stalking and Domestic Terrorism, took several of these cases, and investigated them. What they found differed exponentially from the original police and coroner reports. They presented their cases in the excellent book, "Case Studies in Drowning Forensics."

What they discovered, by thorough re-examination of the cases, including the use of independent pathologists, presented the most chilling of circumstances; and it has not stopped since then; only grown. Even back then, these investigators believed they could tie 100 cases together. A couple of years ago, another organisation called 'Find Me' that I contacted, were also looking into the same phenomenon. Run by ex DEA agent, Kelly Snyder, they said, "That's barely scratching the surface," The figure they quoted was over 300.

When I wrote about the cases in my earlier books, I explained that the two detectives had been joined by Investigative journalist Kristi Piehl, who had found a remarkably suspicious drowning death too, in her town of Minneapolis. Little did she realize there was more than one hundred other similar ones; until she joined forces with the two retired detectives and the Professor.

Very clearly they managed to completely disprove the official findings, and very thoroughly and expertly, they proved that there was nothing accidental or natural at all in these multiple deaths; instead, these young men had very clearly been through the most terrifying ordeals, sometimes lasting weeks, before they were then killed, and taken to the river. Both Senator Sensenbrenner of Wisconsin, and U.S. Congressman McNulty of NY submitted requests to the F.B.I. calling on them to investigate the mounting number, in an effort to make them stop. Instead, however, the cases have continued and show no signs of abating. It is the stuff of nightmares.

Many others began to investigate or follow the cases years ago too, including Vance Holmes, who runs the blog "Drowning in Coincidence," and 'Footprints at the Riversedge,' which is run more as a voice for the families of the victims, as well as 'Killing Killers' which is more of a true crime blog.

Some profilers say it has also spread; that it is happening now in Canada, England and Ireland. Why is it possible to say this? The simple reason is that for anyone looking at them closely enough, there are a lot of recurring similarities in the vast majority of the cases. First mentioned in Book 1 of the 'In the Woods' series, the reason for personally noticing these cases and being drawn to them was because I was researching for a book prior to these, on the subject of Time Travel. This is in some ways unrelated, but it became apparent while researching, that there seemed to be particular areas where there were possible vortexes or dimensional doorways naturally occurring within some forest areas. In these areas, I came across stories of people going missing.

In the Clapham Woods in Sussex, England, a series of disappearances occurred a few years ago. Policeman Peter Goldsmith's body was found hidden amongst the trees in 1972; a Vicar was found dead after disappearing in the forest; then, the body of Jill Matthews was discovered horribly murdered in 1981. Investigators Charles Walker and Toyne Newton believed the woods were being used by a satanic cult, which they claimed was named 'Hecate,' after the goddess of magic and witchcraft.

Charles Walker said that when investigating the strange area, he appealed for information from local people and met with a man in the woods who had contacted him. The man, who stood shrouded by the trees, purposely masking his face, threatened serious repercussions should Walker continue his investigation; claiming that he had the support of some very powerful connections who 'would tolerate no interference' in their ritualistic slaughtering. Walker says mysteriously, "The human disappearances, of which there were several, ended up as "Open verdicts." Searches were made of the likely routes; the paths that these people were thought to have taken and nothing was found...then sometime later, bodies were found, *in areas known to have been extensively searched* by the Police."

In other words, it would seem a possibility that the bodies were kept, either alive or dead, for some time, prior to them being placed back at a spot where they were most likely to be discovered. Echoes of similarity are found in a number of mysterious disappearances in forests, woods, and National Parks across America and Canada. One such area appears to be the Bennington Triangle in the Glastonbury Mountains in Vermont, according to Juanita Baldwin's book '*Disappearances in the Smokey Mountains*,' written twenty years ago, in 1998. This book described the mysterious disappearances of many people, including that of a little boy called Dennis Martin, as well as many adults including Middie Rivers, a deer hunter and professional guide with decades of experience, who inexplicably vanished while escorting a group of hunters.

A 53 year old lady called Frieda Langer also disappeared. She'd got her shoes and socks wet while hiking with her cousin, and had told him to carry on hiking while she returned to their campsite to change her clothing. She said she would then catch him up. She never did catch up with her cousin, and a massive search was instigated. Several months passed by when suddenly she was found, dead, lying on the trail that had been searched multiple times. When looking into this case, according to one newspaper report of the time that I found, when she was found, a witness said her body appeared to be 'fresh,' as though she had just died moments earlier; and yet she had been missing for months. Not only that, but one of the people who came across her body stated that it was like she had been purposely left there to be found, and that her face had 'a look of terror' on it. The implication then was that she had been 'kept' alive somewhere for all of the time she had been missing; killed, and then returned to the woods and 'placed' there.

This reminded me of having listened to Coast to Coast AM a few years back, in 2008, when I was fortunate to catch an episode in which investigative journalist Kristi Piehl described her suspicion regarding the case of a young college-age man in Michigan, who had gone missing only to be found weeks later, dead in the water in the same area in which there had been multiple searches. This reminded me of the Frieda Langer case, and the Clapham Woods cases, and for me, that was when my research turned in the direction of these drowning deaths, and was the reason for describing them in my book series 'Something in the Woods.'

For this young man in Michigan, his death was ruled as drowning, but when Piehl asked an independent pathologist to review the autopsy files, Dr Sikirica concluded that the young man, Todd Geib, had been dead only for a period of between two to five days; not the 4 weeks he had been missing. He also had no water in his lungs; meaning that he did not drown. He had also not been in the water for the extensive time that he had been missing.

The implication became clear that he had been held or kept alive somewhere for almost three weeks prior to being taken to the water in which he was found. He had been placed into the water to make it look like he had drowned.

"These drowning mysteries, they defy logic," she said.

At the same time as this, the two former NYPD detectives, Kevin Gannon and Anthony Duarte were actively trying to figure out how something very similar had happened to more than forty other college-age men across the country. Since then, there have been no answers about why this is happening, and who is doing it. The media have occasionally covered it, but no-where near as much as the families of the dead and missing boys would like. In 2014, Gretchen Carlson covered it. In 2016, Channel 4 in the U.K. covered it. Why would a U.K. TV station cover it? Well, as described in 'Taken in the Woods,' many now feel it has spread to England.

How could this be? And why?

It appears to be escalating. The original detectives believed that whoever is doing this is sending message. But what is the message? What is their motive?

Chapter 5:
Patterns And Links

Many don't buy into the belief that there's something strange going on. They say young men and drinking doesn't go together very well and that accidents are inevitable. Of course, this is a possibility, but when taking a look at some of the cases individually, invariably there will be an element of high strangeness in how and why they ended up dead in the water. When looking at them as a whole too, there is a very clear set of commonalities and patterns which invariably link them together.

How does a person end up dead in water that is only a couple of feet deep? Why can't he get out of that water? Why can he not be found for often what amounts to weeks? Why would he go to the most remote body of water, in the opposite direction to that which he was heading? Why would his cell phone suddenly go dead after he has said something disturbing?

Are there any clues which could help explain what has happened to these young men, and why?

For anyone thinking there is not something very odd going on, perhaps this set of circumstance is a good example for contemplation; Writes a mother, "We almost lost Cullen on Sunday. It all started the night before. He and his friend, Ryan, had gone off to La Cross to the bars, with their friend Jay. My son drove and they all planned to stay the night at Jay's. At 1.30a.m. they were at John's Bar. At 'bar time' Cullen was no-where to be found. Ryan and Jay were trying to find him until 5.30 a.m. Cullen resurfaced at 7.00 a.m. in the Emergency Room of the hospital. He remembers being in the Bar. The next thing he remembers is being in the river. He fought his way out of the river and collapsed on the shore. He had no jacket or shoes. He ran to the sound of the cars nearby, saw a sign for the hospital and ran to the emergency room in just his socks. He voluntarily gave urine and blood samples. I'm thinking he must have had way too much to drink. His results came back; he was not drunk, and yet, he cannot remember anything from 1.30 a.m. until he woke up in the water. What did someone put in his drink? I don't think he realises he almost died. I don't think he realises someone almost killed him. He somehow managed to get out of the water. I think that he *was not drunk* is a factor."

Strangely, he is not the only boy in that area of La Crosse, Wisconsin, to have been in a desperate fight for his life. In the next case however, it ended in tragedy and untold suffering. Jeff Geesy was found drowned in the same river, in 1999. This case was investigated by Gannon and Duarte along with Professor Gilbertson. This young man too had disappeared during a night out in a Bar. He vanished on April 10th. His body was recovered on May 24, in the river.

A bloodhound privately brought in by this team, had tracked the boy's scent to the Niedbalski Bridge, where it had then performed a 'trauma roll,' which was indicative of a physical altercation. It indicted that the boy had undergone a physical altercation of some type. The dog's behaviour then indicated that the boy had been placed into a vehicle and transported from the spot to where his body was recovered. He was found in a shallow gravel pit, drowned. He was missing one shoe, as is often the case. The dog tracked away from the shallow pit however, indicating that someone who had been in physical contact with the boy, had walked away from the area after leaving the body.

Gannon and Gilbertson point out that as this dog tracked the missing boy's scent, it also picked up on another boy's scent; the boy whose mother wrote about what happened to her son, when he found himself running to the hospital in shock and fear that he had somehow got into the river and nearly drowned, yet had no recollection of what had happened to him. He had a lucky escape; but for Jeff Gessy, his body displayed signs that he had been held somewhere, hanging upside down. He had also been drained of blood.

When I spoke to Professor Gilbertson about 3 years ago, he pointed out to me that he was concerned that the deaths appeared to have spread to the U.K. I had also spoken with former federal drug enforcement agent Kelly Snyder's organization, a not-for-profit victim-search group called *Find Me*, composed of active and retired law enforcement officials and consultants. They too had been following the cases from the beginning, and are still investigating them now. "Look at all the names here and we think we've only scratched the surface; that's what's really scary to me,' Snyder said. I had also spoken with several family members of the victims, who were not of the opinion that these were 'accidents.'

When I spoke to Gilbertson in February 2016, he said they had spread to Ireland. Mystery enshrouds so many of these cases and on a side note, when I was first looking into these deaths I was contacted by a person who had a blog dedicated to charting and investigating these deaths. At their own request they asked for anonymity, and warned me that they themselves had come under "extreme psychic and astral attack" while looking into the deaths; so much so that they had been forced to stop. They now wanted nothing more to do with it. They were contacting me to give me a warning. How does psychic astral attack come into this? Later in the book, it will become a lot more evident.

They're not the first one to tell me they had been 'forced' to stop looking into things. Another man actively researching the deaths, JC Smith, has also told me of being 'warned off.' Additionally, although Kristi Piehl appeared on Coast to Coast A.M. a couple of times in an attempt to bring light to these mysterious incidents, it was not long afterward that she too closed down her own blog which was dedicated to investigating the deaths and refused to have any more involvement in the cases. One has to ask then, why people who get involved in this, invariably end up distancing themselves from it? Of course, those who say it is just drunk men falling into water, who have not looked at the circumstances in which they were found, nor the autopsy or police reports, will say it is because they realised it was all something and nothing; that it was drunken accidents; but there are warning signs that keep flagging up for those who attempt to look into it, and this alone causes me to wonder why that would be?

On the other hand, with the continuation of 'footsteps at the riversedge' blog, 'killingkillers' and Vance Holmes' original 'Drowning in Coincidence' blog, on which he tracked the cases from the beginning, it's clear that many others have not stopped looking into it. Are all these people wrong in believing there is a lot more going on than people might realize?

When Kristi Piehl first appeared on Coast to Coast radio back in 2008, she was joined by forensic pathologist Dr Michael Sikirica to discuss the tragic case of one of the victims, Todd Geib. In Casnovia, Michigan, 22 year old

Todd was last seen at a bonfire party in June 2005. It was a marshy rural area. He left the party to walk back alone to his cousin's house, where he lived. He never made it back there. He had called a friend at 12:51 a.m., but all he had said was, "I'm in a field," before the phone call cut off. When the friend rang back, he answered but all the friend could hear was what sounded like the wind.

The area where he was last seen was thoroughly searched three times. During one of the searches, as many as 1,500 volunteers searched the area. Nothing was found. When his body was discovered three weeks later in a remote bed of water, his death was ruled as drowning; however when a new autopsy was carried out, he was discovered to have been dead only 2-5 days, despite being missing for 3 weeks. In other words, he had been somewhere, alive, for approximately two and a half weeks prior to his death. Where he was found had been thoroughly searched at least 3 times.

When the independent pathologist Dr Sikirica was allowed access to the autopsy files, he concluded through forensic analysis that Todd had been dead only between two to five days; and most crucially, he had no water in his lungs; *he could not have drowned,* and his body was not in the condition it would be expected to be in. He had not been in the water for the twenty or so days he had been missing; meaning that he had been held or kept alive somewhere for approximately three weeks, before being taken to the creek.

Dr Sikirica's opinion was backed up by around 200 other examiners, when he presented the case at an international convention of Medical Examiners.
Piehl said of the cases, "A lot of people have asked me, who is doing this? Whoever had Todd, is a sick individual. I think we're going to find a dark human being, of a kind we haven't met yet," said Piehl.

From the investigations of the Ret'd NYPD detectives, Patrick McNeill was the case that first got the attention of the detectives who found the disturbing pattern. He was 21 when he walked out of a bar in New York City on a cold night in February 1997. He told his friends he was taking the subway back to Fordham University. His body was found near a Brooklyn pier nearly two months later. The Pathologist stated he was not drunk when he died of drowning, and two big questions arose. How did he end up dead in the water in Brooklyn? And where had he been for the last two months?

According to Det. Gannon, a car had been seen double parked as the young man exited the Bar he had been drinking in. He appeared very drunk; so much so that he was bending over and uncoordinated. He was clearly feeling nauseous. He attempted to walk off down the street and the double parked car began to move beside him. Patrick stopped as though he was about be sick, stumbled and fell over. The car beside him stopped. When Patrick managed to recover and pick himself back up, the car began to follow him again. He was found more than forty days later, dead in the river.

At his inquest, the Pathologist stated he was not drunk but he died of drowning. Another renowned independent Forensic Pathologist Dr. Cyril Wecht however, when reviewing the case for Kristie Piehl, stated, "There's no way this man is accidentally going to fall into a body of water, (and) the fly larvae (found) have been laid in the groin area. It's an indoor fly—not an outdoor fly. So we have a body that was already dead before it was placed in the water...I would call it a homicide, yes."

In other words, the young man had been kept alive for an extended period of time again, prior to being found in the water; long enough for indoor larvae to settle on his body. He had been kept alive somewhere. Kevin Gannon, investigating the McNeill case since 1997, said, "He was stalked, abducted, held for an extended period of time, murdered, and disposed of."

Chris Jenkins was a very popular student at the University of Minnesota, and he was on the college swim team. He disappeared one night in 2003. When his body was discovered in the Mississippi river four months after he had disappeared, to the police his death looked like an accidental fall after a night of drinking; however, rather disturbingly, his body was found encased in ice, with his hands folded over his chest, in a manner that is wholly inconsistent with the official verdict of drowning. People drowning do not end up in this position. After justified protest from his family, finally after several years, his death was re-classified as 'homicide.'

Honour student Jared Dion, again, like the other boys, was a popular and athletic person. He was discovered, five days after he'd disappeared, in the river near Wisconsin University in 2004. At a later autopsy, it was found that he had been moved ten hours prior to his death, and that because his body was still in rigor, he could not have been dead any longer than 72 hours, meaning he had been alive for some time prior to his death and had not died the day of his disappearance. That left 2 days unaccounted for, which again implied that he had been kept somewhere and placed in the water later. It also implied he could have been drowned elsewhere.

Pathologists don't routinely test if the water found in the lungs is from the same open source water in which they are found; he could have been drowned in a bathtub, or in a van, driven around with a specially made water compartment in the back of it. Jared was dead before he entered the water.

As one anonymous commentator says in a forum; "They are drowned elsewhere and dumped after the

drug is out their system; that's why a lot of the victims are found in areas that have already been searched.
An M.E. isn't always capable of knowing which body of water the victim drowned in. They could all have been drowned in baths; but as the killers seem to be so mobile, I think it's more that they are using a white panel van with a tank of water in the back. - coming from a guy who knows more about these murders than any one living."

Why would he say that last sentence? Is he a phony? Just someone pretending to know what's going on? Or is it really a brag coming from someone either involved, or someone who really does know people who are doing this, and how they are doing it?

Jared had last been seen in a Bar, where he told a friend he was going to a party afterward. He was seen talking to "a blond" but it was never determined if this was a male or female and they have never been identified.
He was found in the opposite direction to which he had told his friend he was heading. He was alive for 3 days after his disappearance. He was drowned, but he didn't drown in the river. He was held, kept alive for three days, drowned, then taken to the river and placed into it.

His autopsy result showed no "pink froth," according to Gannon, and this indicated that there was no struggle to save himself from being drowned. In a struggle to survive while drowning, the blood vessels in the lungs will burst and seep blood into the body; this did not happen when he drowned; there was no struggle.

Bodies have been found in different States at the same time. It cannot possibly be the work of just one man. While it's certainly possible that some of these 300 plus deaths are accidental, or might be victim of murder unrelated to this phenomenon; the overwhelming majority are simply not.

Is it a gang of serial killers? A syndicate of some kind? A cult? An organised group of some kind that has criss-crossed America, travelling to rural college campuses in different cities in a dozen different states in an ever increasing murder spree? It would almost seem as though the men are being deliberately targeted. It's hard to believe that so many educated and sporty men would choose to walk way off their usual route, toward rivers, in the winter, alone, and jump in, or fall in. Why are the bodies returned to the area previously searched? Is it abductor/abductors? Or is it something less easy to define?

Some have commented that the victims clothes have been tampered with prior to being found, sometimes being put back on their bodies the wrong way, suggesting that they were removed by someone. What does this imply?

Most likely it is the work of some kind of organized gang. This is the belief of gang stalking expert Professor Gilbertson. That is his opinion, based on thorough scrutiny of the individual cases, the identical victim type, and what he believes is their abduction, confinement and subsequent death by drowning.

But why death by drowning? Why this particular method of killing? We will get to that in a short while; and it makes for very disturbing reading.

When I was talking to Professor Gilbertson, he raised concerns that the unexplained phenomenon of identikit young men ending up dead seemed to have spread to England too. Professor Gary Jackson, head of Psychology at the University of Birmingham, England has also officially joined the growing number of people who are perturbed, alarmed, and feel there is something more sinister at play than accidental drowning after more than 85 men in the last five years have been found dead in the canals and ponds of the Northern City of Manchester. Talking to the broadsheet The Telegraph, he says, "The number is far higher than one would expect and from the data I just don't believe these were suicides; canals are not a popular site for suicide, and people rarely choose this for their method; but they make for ideal grounds for predators. Many of the reports from the coroners are inconclusive."

Professor Jackson, having accessed freedom of information reports regarding many of the deaths, has come to a grim conclusion. He doesn't believe they were accidents. Pointedly he adds, "If you're trying to commit suicide by drowning, it's very hard to do in a canal - unless you can weigh yourself down with something heavy."

Some of the deaths it seems have clearly indicated that something else might be going on other than an innocent accidental fall into the canals. He also points to the very clear victimology - they were all young males. He says there is a clear connection between the cases from the fact that the in at least 48 of the cases, the bodies were so badly decomposed as to be impossible to identify. This links them together connectively in his opinion. If these victims were being randomly pushed in by someone vindictive, they would not all be successful attempts. At some point, one of the victims would fight, struggle, and not drown. People would soon hear about it. No-one has come forward to say this has happened to them, although doubtless the dark and dimly lit canals are excellent places for drug deals, and muggings.

If they were all cases of criminal attempts and 'success' by psychopathic muggers, why is it not happening in Cambridge, another University town with canals, or Universities by the sea, of which there are many, such as Bournemouth or Brighton? Not only that, but with Newspaper reports carrying images of police teams being able to walk through some stretches of the canals because the water is not even knee deep, it does beg the question how could they all so easily drown in shallow water? The canals of Manchester run through parts of the city centre, mainly the old industrial parts but also quite close to very busy nightclubs and bars. Manchester is both a thriving University town and has a popular Gay Village, and every night, bars are packed with drinkers.

Many will inevitably on occasion drink too much, some will as a result have accidents; however, the canals are not obvious routes to take. They are not renovated scenic canals; rather they are dimly lit, strewn with litter and damp. They aren't a short cut to anywhere and they aren't a route home. They're not somewhere anyone would go for a pleasant walk. Yet some of the deaths have clearly indicated that something else might be going on other than an innocent accidental fall into the canals. No-where near where he lived or where he had been drinking.

One link that really stands out, as previously discussed in '*Taken in the Woods*', is that very often the young men who go missing have been kicked out of clubs and bars and left to wander the streets often without the means of getting home. Often their coats have been left inside the bars, with their keys and wallets inside. There is also very often the common factor that they have been talking on their cell phones when their calls have suddenly been cut off.

With reference to the victim's being kicked out of the bars, is this case of negligence of duty of care in the case of doormen? Or is there something more sinister going on in terms of collusion and cooperation between them and the as yet unknown and unidentified gang allegedly stalking and abducting these men?

In several cases afterward, it has been found that although the young men were kicked out, there was no evidence of them causing a disturbance or fight, or even being that drunk. In other words, there was no real reason to throw them out. A reason seems to have been *created*.

Take the case of Shane Montgomery, a student at West Chester who was escorted out of a Bar in Manayunk, PA, on Thanksgiving 2014, after accidentally tripping into the dj deck. His body was found 5 weeks later in a part of the river close to the bar where search divers had thoroughly and repeatedly searched. The implication here then being that he was not in the river for all of the time that he had been missing. He was also found in water just three to four feet deep, which would seem a little shallow to drown in surely? Unusually in this case, the FBI quickly became involved in the investigation searching for him, and some have asked why they got involved. Curiously, it has since been reported that the bar involved stated that there was no disturbance inside the bar and he was not escorted out.

Nick Wilcox was out celebrating the New Year in 2013, in Milwaukee. His girlfriend later said that they had met some new people in the bar, had hung out with them, and that when Nick was kicked out of the Bar, one of the new crowd, a young man, had left with him. By the time she was able to get outside of the packed bar to join him, he had disappeared.

A medical examiner's report indicated he was found about 350 to 500 feet from where he was last seen, and cell phone records obtained by police show the last "ping" on his phone was close to where his body was discovered. Wilcox was found with his cell phone, a set of keys and his wallet, containing his driver's license. He had been missing more than 80 days yet he was found less than 500 feet from where he had disappeared. Bodies surface in water within about 10 days usually. Where had his body been? It couldn't have been in that water. His family do not believe what happened to him was an 'accident.'

28 year old Thomas Hecht also disappeared in Milwaukee, on the 10th of March 2012, after joining his friends in the St Patrick's Day Pub Crawl. His body wasn't found in the river for nearly two weeks. He lived within walking distance of the Bar, which he left at just after 9 p.m. He never made it back to his apartment.

Chapter 6:
The Phone Calls

Why do many of them make desperate phone calls just moments before something happens to them? Why are some of them in such a state of terror or horror as they phone their parents or friends? And why does their phone then go dead? What are they seeing, in the moments before their phone is cut off?

In January 2016, the U.K.'s Channel 4 aired a documentary looking into the drowning phenomenon that has taken on a pattern in the area of Manchester and its bodies of water. Not only have young men been found drowned in the canals in the City, but also in bodies of water and rivers around the city edge.

One previously mentioned in 'Taken in the Woods,' the case of David Plunkett, was featured into the documentary. The police are saying that the near to 90 cases of dead men is down to them drowning and are as a result of no suspicious circumstances.

Perhaps that is the case; perhaps as others are saying, there is a serial killer, who, in the absence of the identity of this figure, has been given the nickname, 'The Pusher.' Profilers I have been in contact with over the years however fear that it is a replication of the drowning deaths as seen in the United States.

They believe this phenomenon is not constrained to a small geographical area but is spread internationally and is operated by groups of geographically located 'cells;' like Terrorists organise themselves, but these are not 'terrorists' as we would normally understand them to be.

David Plunkett, just like the majority of the U.S. victims, died in inexplicable circumstances. In February 2015, David's friend called David's parents to explain that he had lost David, and wanted to know if they had heard form him. His friend said that David had been 'kicked out' of the event for allegedly being intoxicated.

David and his friend had been attending a music event at the racetracks in the city centre. His mother reassured his friend that she would call David herself and find out where he was. When her son answered her call, at first she heard only silence, and what sounded like him walking somewhere very quiet. Then, after a few minutes, while the call was still connected, he suddenly began to howl. His mother described it as a horrific sound, "unearthly" and utterly chilling.

"I couldn't get through to him. He couldn't talk. He couldn't tell me where he was. A good 7-8 minutes into the call there was suddenly this ghastly screaming. I started crying."

Unable to get him to listen to her, she passed the phone to her husband while she dialled the police in their landline phone.

His father too could not get him to listen to him, to tell him what was going on or where he was. "I raised my voice to get him to snap out of it but I couldn't get through to him. He couldn't talk. We couldn't help him. Then there was total silence."

Neither could the police; because David was unable to stop screaming. His body was found three weeks later in the city canal. His mother has later said that she can only understand that he must have seen something so terrifying.

The distraught parents of the young man went to the Newspapers to speak out about their distress, caused by having to endure listening to their son screaming down the phone to them in the last moments of his life. The police later traced his phone to a location two miles outside of the city; in an area David had no reason to be heading to and wouldn't even have been familiar with. His phone was found as though 'placed' on the path beside the canal. His glasses too were found there beside the phone.

A former murder detective from Scotland Yard was hired for the TV documentary makers to investigate his and two other young men found drowned. What the detective couldn't understand was why David would have gone to that location, voluntarily. The route to the canal where he was said to have entered the water was down a small dark side road that appeared to be a dead-end.

The detective also could not fathom how the coroner and police had established that he must have fallen into the water accidently, when in order to do that, he would have had to scale a high fence. They said that he had slipped down the embankment and into the water and that was why he had screamed.

If he had slipped and fallen in, disregarding for a moment that he would have had to get back up after falling down and then climb over a high fence, it's entirely he could have screamed out in surprise and shock; but he wouldn't have howled continually for the length of several minutes.

Reminiscent of David's case, is that of Henry McCabe's in Minnesota. He left the most horrifying voicemail on his brother's phone in the early hours after he too had disappeared. A kayaker later discovered his body in Rush Lake, Minnesota, on November 2nd, 2015. The location was seven miles from where he had been dropped off by a friend after a night out, according to the local News Fox9 reports. There are several strange factors in this case.

Searchers acknowledged that the location in which he was found had previously been searched by them, after they had extended the search grid. They had not found his body when they had searched there before, and yet the local law enforcement said the victim appeared to have been *half in and half out* of the water there "for some time."

Part of the voicemail is on several news sites on the internet. Listening to it is one of the most chilling experiences imaginable, and the horror that the man is going through is unspeakable. Newspapers reporting on it described it as, "two minutes of undecipherable noises, including what sound like growls and moans of pain."

The words don't encapsulate the sheer terror the man is experiencing. Even worse is when his screams, growls and cries are interrupted by a voice, so cold and detached, that tells him simply; "Stop it."

There appears to be strange sounds in the background, perhaps machinery, although it is also possible that it is Mr McCabe making those sounds, as he is both screaming and growling in evident agony. It's the most chilling, most disturbing thing I have ever heard.

Is it possible that he too was a victim of this organized group? The voice in the recording telling him to stop screaming is chilling in itself for the sheer calmness with which it is said. It's a said by a very calm person, who is not out of control or in any kind of frenzied state, which would be the norm if it was a very personal revenge-style killing, or a killing by a very mentally disturbed individual.

This person on the voicemail however, is only calm, detached and cold. The voice is not panicked, or screaming back at him. He is completely neutral, as though it is nothing shocking to him; as though it's something he is very used to doing, as though it's the sort of thing he does everyday.

Most bizarrely, the police said at the time that they were "unable to make any definite conclusions about the disturbing voicemail."

His body was found after multiple searches; so the question is, where had he been in the days he'd been missing? The official statement was that he appeared to have been in the water "for some time," but what water was that?

It doesn't mean, as we have seen from other earlier examples, that he was dead in that water or drowned in that water. It could have been water somewhere else; and that is why it is so creepy. Why drown a person in water, water which could even be a bathtub or shower in a house, or a tub of water in a mobile van, and then move them to another place of water, once dead?

As Gannon and Gilbertson point out in their book 'Case Studies in Drowning Forensics,' pathologists do not ordinarily necessarily check to see what type of water they drowned in; particularly when the discovery of the body in water to them clearly illustrates that they have drowned in it. They don't then necessarily test water samples from that river to make sure it matches the water in the victim's lungs; and then there are the cases where no water is found in their lungs anyway, when a second pathologist takes a look at the pathologist report.

Both the police and the Medical Examiner for Ramsey County reported that McCabe's death "does not look suspicious." His body has no signs of trauma. The authorities are said to be waiting for toxicology results.

Henry perhaps does not fit the 'usual' profile of this group of killers. He was older, at the age of 32, and was not a college student. It could very easily turn out to be foul play on the part of his friends, or enemies he may have had, or even a random attack. Where it does fit the pattern however, is that once again, he made a telephone call in distress and absolute terror.

Once again, his body was found a long time after the attack, in a remote body of water, in an area way out of the last place he was seen. Added to this is the belief of some profilers that these killers have extended their repertoire.

Henry McCabe also fits the profile of Gannon; "these young men are being abducted by individuals, held for a period of time before they're entered into the water. These victims are mentally tortured and sometimes physically tortured, prior to being killed."

Mental torture certainly applied here; and yet the strange thing is, how did he appear to be in so much pain that he was screaming for two minutes of the call and yet have no marks of trauma on his body?

How is someone mentally tortured by what ever it is that is being done to them, something so bad that it sounds as though they are being physically gutted, and yet there are no marks?

Henry was reportedly last seen by 'an acquaintance' who told authorities that they had been to a nightclub prior to the horrific voicemail. This acquaintance then said that he had dropped the victim off at a gas station with a convenience store, close to the nightclub, at just after 2 a.m. It seems that was the last time anyone saw Henry alive. It was approximately thirty minutes later when he made the blood-curdling telephone call.

His body was discovered more than a month later in a remote bed of water, in a river that had been searched many times. Local investigators believe that when he made the call he was in the area of Rice Creek Park, on the border of the New Brighton community, although the area was subsequently thoroughly searched and they could find no trace of him.

He was a tax auditor working for the Department of Revenue. So far, nothing in his personal life nor professional life has given any indication of who may have been involved in his disappearance; although the accuracy of his 'acquaintance's' statement about where he was dropped off has been questioned, because Henry was found in such a different location, but there are no indications that the police have any suspects in mind at all among those who knew him. There were three pings from his cell phone, showing that they had come from three separate locations in the early hours that he went missing. Is it possible that he could have moved around so far on foot? Or had he been bundled into a van, like many of the other victims quite possibly appear to have been.

Jeff Geesy for example, was determined to have been placed into a vehicle by the tracker dog. Chris Jenkins, as previously discussed, was also determined to have been placed into a vehicle by the tracker dogs who were brought in by his family to try to solve how he had vanished outside a Bar.

Student Daniel Zamlen was reported as a missing person on April 5th 2009. He'd been at a party but his friends who were at the party said that he had left on his own to meet up with another friend at Minnesota University. They say he was talking with them on his cell phone and was near the Mississippi River Boulevard and St Clair Avenue. Quickly bloodhounds, a helicopter and searchers covered the area where he had been walking, but found no trace of him. Bloodhounds seemed to get partial hits on his scent near the river, but his father maintains that they kept stopping in the same place, and did but did not actually go near the river. He also said that his own job was as an open pit miner and he understood land, and when he walked that area, he did not believe that someone could just accidently slip into the water there; but if they did, he said it would have left marks and none were found.

In what is one of the most disturbing phone calls, reminiscent of the call received by the parents in Manchester, his friend Anna says she was talking to him when he began to become distressed? By then she says she had left the party and got in her car to go and find him.

'It took a really bad turn,' she told newspapers at the time, "Where are you?" she asked him.
"Oh, my gosh, Help!" – "This was the last thing I heard," she says. "His voice became distant as he said those words, as though he was moving away his phone, and then the line went dead."
She called him back but it just remained unanswered she claims.
It has to be said, his parents have spoken out about the accuracy of statements made by his friends, particularly disputing the content of his last known call.

Disturbingly his Mother also reported that there's significant evidence the drinks at the party had been spiked. His body was found a month later in the river. A baseball was found near the scene with a smiley face on it, as well as a sign that was marked with smiley face graffiti near the edge. It was discovered that some of the drinks at the party had been laced with the drug GHB.

His mother has stated "Victims of drowning usually surface within six and ten days after the drowning. The River was flowing four hundred times faster than normal yet Dan's body didn't surface for another 27 days and flowed only two miles."

She says, "The Coroner could not determine 100% that he did drown; just that that was where he was found."

Crucially, she also reports that the night before he disappeared, he was at a Club in the centre of town. He was thrown out because he was not wearing the right wristband. She says, "He was separated from his friends and later he told his friends that he was approached by men outside. He said that he "ran" from these people. Sound familiar? Maybe he was supposed to have his 'tragic accident' that night, but even though "very intoxicated" he was able to out run these people."

Very strangely, a keyword search online leads to something found on 'Plaintxt;' a website described as 'a huge database of questions and answers on any topics, supported by links to independent sources. Here you can ask your questions...'

And it appears the question asked was,
'What is the complete address of the man dan zamlen? [...] drop-off points for city, province, postal code [...]'

It was dated 2009. There was nothing else on the website accompanying this. Is this again meaningless? A false lead and just something entirely unrelated? Or is there any possibility that it was indeed a pre-planned action, a plan to target him before he even knew he had become a target? Before the night it happened to him?

Student Brandon Swanson, of Marshall, Wisconsin, disappeared in a field in May 2008, after his phone call got cut off to his Father who was out looking for him.
"It didn't sound like he'd fallen over or tripped; it sounded like he was shocked by something; horrified even."

Brandon has never been found. Tracker dogs went to the canal where he had last been known to have been, out in the rural fields and farmland, but they tracked away from the water across a field; where his scent suddenly stopped.

A swear word uttered in what was both surprise and shock was the last thing his father heard, ending a fifty minute telephone call as his father kept him on the telephone, trying to find him. His son had called him late that evening to say he'd run his car into a dried mud bank and couldn't get it out; it was stuck and he'd asked his parents to come and get him. It was May 2008 and student Brandon had been driving home to Marshall in Minnesota; a rural and mainly agricultural county comprised mainly of canals and wind projects. In fact, he'd just completed a technical college course in wind turbines.

After waiting for a while for his parents to turn up he became impatient when they told him on the phone that they were having trouble locating him. He told them he was going to walk toward the nearest town, whose lights he said were in the distance and said that he expected them to meet him en-route. However, it would seem that perhaps Brandon was slightly off in his description of where he thought he was, because no matter how hard his parents looked for him, they couldn't locate him or his car.

He continued walking on toward the lights in the distance as his parents searched for him, now well after midnight, and they stayed in contact throughout, with his Father keeping him talking on the telephone. Brandon was certain he knew where he was and he couldn't understand why his parents couldn't find him and he was becoming increasingly irritated; yet his parents had gone to exactly where he said he was and he was definitely not there. They continued to drive around the roads, unable to see him or his car, and then came the swear word in which he sounded suddenly surprised and shocked, and the phone cut off.

It didn't sound like he had fallen over or tripped up; it sounded like he was shocked by something, even horrified by something; but by what?

Whatever it was, Brandon did not answer his telephone again, despite his father constantly calling his number back. Now his parents were concerned. He wasn't answering his phone for some reason and they had no idea what had just happened to him, where he was, or what might be happening to him still.

Desperately they continued to drive around, urgently trying to find his location, and get him to answer his phone, and in fact they proceeded to spend several hours that early morning desperately looking for him, yet still they failed to spot any sign of him. Around dawn they called the police and a search for the missing student was immediately initiated. It wasn't until the following day that the police were able to locate his missing car, by tracing signals received at cell phone towers from his cell phone.

The car was in fact nearly twenty miles from the town the boy had thought he'd been heading toward on foot. He'd told his parents that he was close to the town when he'd called them to come get him. That was why they couldn't find him that night. He'd been nearly twenty miles away from where he thought he was. He'd thought that the lights he could see on the horizon were the town but he was wrong, he was many miles from the town, and so while his parents had gone to that location, he had been wandering around miles away from them. That explained why they couldn't find him, but it didn't explain why he could not be found now. The search party could not find him, or his cell phone.

What investigators started to believe was that he'd accidentally walked into and then fallen into the river as he was talking to his father. That could explain his shock, they thought. His father wasn't convinced. He said he may have had a drink, and according to the friends he'd been with that evening, he had been drinking but definitely not enough for him to have been drunk, and his father said he didn't sound drunk throughout the phone conversation that lasted almost an hour. It didn't seem plausible that he could fall in and not get out.

Despite an exhaustive search of both the water and the land however, he could not be found. Searchers said the river was flowing fast at the time and could have swept him away, but the water was extensively searched and they could not find his body. The searches included aerial searches, horseback, ATV and many friends and volunteers on foot. They looked repeatedly over the ground. After the official searches ended, his family, along with volunteers didn't give up however, and continued to look for him for weeks.

The only clue came from the K9 search dogs that seemed to indicate that his scent had travelled in one particular direction, but that did not lead to finding his body as the scent stopped. However perhaps that was a clue that he couldn't have gone in the water after all. What did hamper the search efforts, particularly the ability to track his scent, is that the area by its geographical nature is one of criss-crossing winds that break up the flow of scent.

It was possible that he'd succumbed to hypothermia, especially if he'd walked through wet grass and been out in the cold for hours, but it was May, not winter, and even so, they still should have been able to find his body.

Did his call, which ended so abruptly in shock, indicate that he had somehow become the victim of foul play? Had someone arrived there at the scene? Had they abducted him? Was that why his body was never found?

His heartbroken mother talked to news channels after the incident. "He wasn't injured. He said he was ok, no damage to his car. He felt confident about where he was and he was saying that we were lost. The minute

the call dropped I became sick. I knew; I knew it was wrong and I knew it was bad."
Brandon Swanson is still missing.

A man with a very similar name, Brandon Lawson, a 27 year old male who was living in Bronte Texas, also made a desperate phone call before he disappeared. He was just off the highway outside of Bronte when he called the police. It was August 2013 and just after midnight. He'd gone for a drive to get some time to himself, leaving his wife and children at home. Shortly after, he ran out of gas and he phoned his brother and wife to ask them to come and bring him some gasoline. While awaiting their arrival however, something happened that's hard to understand. He made a desperate 911 call.

It's on YouTube to listen to, and many have tried to decipher exactly what he said. It sounds like he tells the police dispatcher he's run out of gas and that he's hiding in the woods just off the highway. It's hard to understand his exact words in the 911 call, but many who have heard it believe it's something along these lines;
"I got chased into the woods," or "There's guys chasing me in the woods."
Then he says what sounds like; "Pushed some guy over. I accidently ran into them. I'm not speaking to them. I'm in the middle of a field. I ran into somebody.

There's a car here. Got taken through the woods. Please hurry, please help."

He says to the dispatcher, "When I talked to them I told them I need to go."

She replies, "Ah, so you ain't into them, ok."

Or, he is saying that he ran into some guys, he has hold of one of them, but they took another man or a boy into the woods.

He's out of breath and distressed. Then his voice disappears from the call and the dispatcher is left asking him if he's still there. She gets no reply.

Because the call doesn't make complete sense in the flow of what he says, it could probably also be concluded that he's either disorient, scared, or in shock.

He mentions other cars, other people, but again it's very hard to decipher. Who were the other guys? What was going on?

That night, there was a lot of confusion. The police didn't turn up, despite him saying he needed the police and telling them to hurry, in fear of his own safety. A state trooper did arrive at the truck by chance, seeing it abandoned while he was driving by, but this was unrelated to the 911 call. His brother and his wife also arrived on the scene with a gas can.

Brandon made another call to his brother while they were standing with the Trooper, but the signal was really bad and his brother could barely hear what was being said. He did hear the words, "I'm in a field," and that Brandon said he was bleeding, but his brother assumed he was hiding out from the police because he'd just learnt he had an outstanding minor warrant. His brother didn't hear him properly on the phone, and wasn't aware of just how desperate the situation as that his brother was facing.

Neither his brother and wife, nor the Trooper was aware of his first call for help to the 911 dispatchers. Since then there has been no sign of him. He has not been seen since. The next day his family and the state troopers began searching for him when it was understood that he hadn't returned home.

An aerial search with infrared and a grid foot search were carried out. Later, cadaver dogs were brought in, but nothing was found of the man. Texas SAR did thorough and extensive searches in the area looking for any sign of him, in case he had got lost and lay injured, or had died out there. According to his wife however, his last cell phone ping was received three miles from the area, and perhaps outside of the area at first searched. However, he still has not been found. No body, no clothes, no car keys or wallet; no trace of him.

His disappearance is truly a mystery, as is who was with him and possibly chasing him that night. He said in the 911 call that he was being chased by men in the woods. Who were the men and why were they chasing him?

When the Trooper and his brother arrived at his truck there were no other cars or trucks pulled over beside his. His own truck showed no signs of a collision or accident, so when he said he "ran into them," he didn't mean that he had an accident while in the car.

What does seem likely is that if he called 911 for help, he wasn't in fact hiding from the Cops in the woods. He'd called them himself asking for help. Some have speculated that it was maybe a cop who was taking a man or the men through the woods. If that were the case however, would he then call the cops and run the risk of other cops turning up, ones that knew the cop in the woods and may well be in on whatever bad thing was going down.

Where did the car go that he said was near him when he called 911? Where did the men go? Why were they chasing him? What did they do to him? If he was bleeding, as he told his brother, why did the search dogs not pick up on his blood scent?

Todd Geibb, one of the first cases noticed by Kristi Piehl, and retired detectives Kevin Gannon and Anthony Duarte, as having the strange set of circumstances where a young man goes missing, makes a final phone call, and is then found dead in water at a later time period. Todd had left a bonfire party in rural Casnovia,

Michigan in June 2005, to go home. At 12.51 a.m he called a friend. He said to them, "I'm in a field," then his phone cut off.

His friend called back but heard either breathing or the wind, but no voice. Further attempts to reach his friend failed. Todd was found three weeks later in a remote bed of water that had been previously searched three times by more than 1500 people. A couple out walking saw his body, sticking half out of the water in an unnatural position, his head and shoulders above the water. It appeared as though he had been placed for a specific reason; as though placed there to be found.

An independent pathologist disagrees with the official autopsy; as did two hundred other pathologists. All of these pathologists determined that he did not die in the water and his body had not been in the water for the three weeks he had been missing. He had been dead only from 2-5 days. The original ex-detectives firmly believe they found evidence of very similar cases taking place in other parts of the country, on the same day.

Tommy Booth was found in the river on February 3rd, 2008, in Woodlyn, Pennsylvania. Video surveillance shows him and his friends entering the doors of 'Bootleggers' nightclub fifteen nights earlier. No-one ever saw him leave, just like the case of promising Med. Student Brian Shaffer, who disappeared in an upstairs bar in the South Campus Gateway, in Ohio in

2006. No-one saw him leave either; and no scent could be tracked. Brian Shaffer is still missing.

Tommy Booth's fate however was determined when he was found in a thawed river two weeks after he disappeared. His body had been positioned in the river into a certain spot in the water by the use of two small sticks. His body however bore no signs of trauma. Crucially, according to the retired detectives and profiler working on his case, independently of the official investigation, they discovered that the young man's cell phone had been purposely 'blocked' so that it couldn't receive a signal, after he went missing.

22-year-old Josh Snell vanished in June, 2005, in Eau Claire. His brother later told reporters he'd been in town to attend a wedding and that afterward, his brother had gone with friends to some bars in town. Four days later his brother's body was pulled from the Chippewa River. His brother said he does not believe his brother 'just wandered into the water.'

He went missing on the same day as Todd Geib, and Josh's last contact seems to have been when he called a friend late that night with a disturbing message. In the phone call, his brothers says, "he said he was scared, that he was hiding in some brush, that he was running from someone. He said he didn't know who it was, or how he was going to get away. He said he didn't do anything, but he was terrified and he was scared for his life."

Another source close to him quotes, "He called a friend to say that he thought unknown people were following him and that he might be in trouble with the police." The Local police said they had no contact with Snell however.

Are these young men being hunted via their cell phones? Chosen somehow and tracked via the signals given out from their cell phones? Are their cell phones then being jammed somehow, like Tommy Booth's was? What do the police have to do with these cases? Or, are there men pretending to be cops in some of these cases? What are these men seeing in the last moments before they end their calls, or their calls are ended for them?

S. Ward's brother also died in very mysterious and very suspicious circumstances. "He was last seen alive at Landsharks Bar, Indianapolis, with a 'bouncer' at approximately 1:30 a.m. on October 12, 2012. His last attempt to save his own life was at 1:30 am when he dialled 911 from his Phone for help. His killers interrupted his 911 call and murdered him...He knew he was going to be killed."

"His desperate call lasted for 1-second, which was just enough to register to the nearest cell phone tower...but it wasn't not long enough to save his life. That was the last time we know him to be alive, until the Construction workers discovered his body on October 22, 2012, floating in the River a few blocks from the bar (less than a mile) 10 days after his desperate call to 911 that night. His phone was found on the bank of the River behind a Restaurant. The police said he must have been 'drunk', 'fallen in' or 'gone swimming' in the dead of winter."

Interviewed by crime writer, Eponymous Rox of the Killing Killers Blog Spot, his mother said, "Where he was found, the depth was two feet. He was going (to the Bar) to meet a young woman he'd been talking with on OkCupid.com dating website. She didn't show up. She said she was from Brownsburg, Indiana. He said that she was in college and planning to become a lawyer. One odd thing that he mentioned about her was that she told him she'd got a college scholarship for wrestling. Looking into this, I have not been able to find any school that has a women's wrestling program. The Indianapolis PD did not question her and still have not had their cyber unit complete that part of the investigation."

"He had met up with her in the week prior to the night (he disappeared) and said that she'd come to meet him with a few friends, to make it more of a laid-back group. They were not going on a dinner-type date, it was more of a casual situation where they could hang out and get to know each other. It seemed to make sense that she was probably being cautious, as a young woman meeting up with a man that she met online. That Friday night, I understood that he would be meeting her and her same friends he'd met the other night."

His mother's testimony would appear to offer a couple of very intriguing possibilities; while a glance at college scholarships offered for women at colleges shows there are some, the statistics given of the percentage of female high school Wrestlers who go on to compete in college is just 3%. That's a tiny number. In a post on IndianaMat.com, which is a place 'to give people involved with wrestling in the state of Indiana promotion,' there's a post which says, "I'm a coach for Brownsburg MS (the area which the girl online said she was in school) My 8th grader is looking for scholarship opportunities. I was wondering if you have any advice?" It would seem then that they are not easy to come by then perhaps?

It was an online correspondence initially between the girl wrestler and the victim, until they met in person. Was it really a woman he was talking to, or was it perhaps a man pretending to be a woman who had been corresponding with him, who had slipped up when he said he had a wrestling scholarship? Is this a vital clue of a 'group' involvement? If so;why?

And if so, who is behind this group? It's extremely unlikely that a young group like this could be planning and carrying out nationwide abductions and murders, Remembering that sometimes young men have gone missing in different states in the same manner on the same night; were this group who showed up the first time to meet her son, somehow recruited to play a key role, possibly like some of the bouncers too?

His date and her friends never showed up. While he was seen in other bars in the street and on CCTV in the bars, and while he left alone, his father says to journalist Eponymous Rox, "I believe he was murdered on the basis of his 911 call being at 1:40 am, terminated within a second. He was in excellent physical condition, capable of getting out of three feet of water, and, he was visiting from California and was not familiar with the area and accessible paths to the canal." (In other words, his father means, why would he have gone down to the canal if he didn't even know it was there?)

His mother says, "My conclusion is someone, (probably more than one) was with him. It's very suspicious and illogical that a very healthy, strong, trained athlete 'fell' and drowned in three feet of water on his own."

The same family has also written an article on their website, dedicated to the mystery of their own son's death, with regards to another young man. "Coincidence?" they ask, of the circumstances surrounding the death of another boy, Joshua Swalls, (whose Toxicology reports later came back to show that he was not drunk nor under the influence of recreational drunks) when the 22 year old also vanished, not far from where their son did, and was subsequently found dead three weeks later in a retention pond that had already been searched by police divers after he went missing.

He disappeared three weeks after their son, and had vanished from outside of a friend's apartment, leaving his car keys, wallet and phone inside. Ward's family say, "So now there are 2 men that go missing within 3 weeks and 2 miles of each other and are later found dead in bodies of water. Obviously, the police have to consider the possibility that something is wrong here, right? Wrong. The police say again; a case of "drunk and fell in."

However, that night Josh had not had anything to drink before going to his friend's apartment. He stayed just over 35 minutes and did drink at his friends, but as the later autopsy shows, he didn't have enough alcohol in his system to be classified as drunk. The biggest problem his family see is how and why the young man managed to get to where he did.

Ward's family too say, "To get into that pond, he would have to scale a 6 foot fence. How then, after he had enough coordination and presence of mind to figure out how to get into that pond, did he become so incapacitated that he didn't realize he was walking into freezing water and suddenly forgot how to swim? Does this not sound crazy to anyone else?"

Matthew Ward's Toxicology results came back clean. He was also a semi-pro Muy Thai fighter.

In this case, in March 2006, an Ohio med student was having drinks with friends to celebrate Spring break. During the evening he called his girlfriend to tell her he was looking forward to the trip they were going to take in a couple of day's time. In the bar he was seen on the security camera at the top of the elevator, but then he moves out of shot. That was the last time he was seen. An emergency exit was covered by camera; he was not picked up on that either.

The only other route would have been to walk through an area of new construction, although tracker dogs did not detect his scent on searching that area. He has still not been found. Brian Shaffer seems almost to have vanished from inside a bar. Despite there being 3 surveillance cameras capturing all people entering and leaving the bar, he was not seen leaving.

Observers have suggested, 'Something else took him right in that bar.'

Chapter 7:
The Suspects

Not only is it happening Statewide, but it probably goes back way before before this. In 1997, Charles Blatz, a student at Wisconsin Plateville Campus, had gone to the yearly Oktobersfest. This is a common factor; many times, the young men disappear on public holidays, like Halloween, New Year's Day, Labor Day, or festival days. There are also many times when the young men disappear on their birthdays; both of these occasions are admittedly opportunities for perhaps getting more drunk than usual, because they are celebrating.

However, it's also the perfect time to approach strangers. On a birthday or holiday, people's guards are down more, people are more open to mingling and partying with strangers; for the very reason that they are having a celebration. This is quite possibly a very obvious way that the 'killers' are targeting and selecting their prey.

Charles had only recently left the military, with an honourable discharge. He was an older student, at the age of 28. It was September 27th and he was in a Bar called Sneakers. ('sneakers' footwear may have an obvious meaning, given that many are found missing a shoe. Other times, just one sneaker is found at the scene.)

The Bar was a popular one downtown and at a short time after midnight he left. Five days later his body was pulled out of the Mississippi River. One of his sneakers was no longer on his feet. Forty eight hours later, Anthony Skifton, aged 19, went missing. He had last been seen as he left a party, carrying a pack of beer. Five days later his body was spotted in Swift Creek. Four months passed. Then 20 year old Nathan Kapfer, a student at Viterbo College, a private Roman Catholic University in La Crosse, Wisconsin, was kicked out of a bar for being intoxicated.

Nathan was not happy with this, and the police were called to the scene. He was arrested and taken to the police station. At just past 2 a.m. however, he was released from custody. After that, he vanished. It was to be a month and a half before he was found, dead in the river. His baseball cap however had been found long before this, along with his wallet and the citations the police had given him. They were all neatly arranged on the deck of a shop beside the rivers edge.

The police believed this was a possible indication he had committed suicide. Others were not so convinced of this. Then Jeff Geesy disappeared, as has already been described earlier. He was found in the river, his body completely drained of blood, as determined not by the first official autopsy, which failed to mention this, but by a private autopsy arranged by the original retired detectives.

It was also evident that he'd been hanging upside down for at least 10 hours prior to his death, which had occurred shortly before he was placed in the water, despite being missing for more than 40 days.

As for Nathan, two days after he was reported missing, a local resident reported to the police that he had seen a young man of the same age group and appearance as Nathan, standing on a bridge in the day time, staring down into the water, "oblivious to everything."

Of course, the easy answer is that he committed suicide, but his girlfriend said he had spoken of those who took their own lives, saying it was a selfish cop-out. She didn't believe he had drowned himself. His Father too said, he wasn't the type to do that, and added, "I can't believe these kids just fell in or jumped in."

Of course, as will later be discussed, there are several reasons why someone could appear to be completely oblivious to everything, as though in a 'trance.' Nathan's body was also found in the river more than 40 days after he went missing.

The Police Lieutenant, Dan Marcou, spoke publicly after that, to appeal to local residents not to buy into this idea that young men were being killed and then placed in the water; he was the Uncle of one of the boys who had been found dead in the river. He wanted the theory put to bed.

Wisconsin University too wanted it quashed. Betsy Morgan, Chair of the Psychology department at the University there, along with criminologist Kim Vogt, also spoke out to dispel the belief that a predatory lone wolf serial killer was picking off young men at random.

While the victims were all of the same demographic and characteristics, they pointed out that this had a lot to do with the naturally occurring homogeny of the area; mainly white students. There was no physical evidence, they said, and they were of the belief that drowning was a risky and not necessarily guaranteed method of killing people.

They also said that serial killers prefer up-close killing so that they could enjoy watching it. They did entertain the idea that hypothetically the young men could be drowned in a bathtub after being sedated by a drug, and then taken to the river and disposed of; but at the same time they said this was a highly unlikely scenario. On the other hand, criminal psychologist Dr M. Godwin stated, "The probability that five students just happened to end up in the River is zero."

An independent expert on serial homicide with sexual deviancy, Ms. Pat Brown, also joined in the debate. In fact, she went further than all of them in her involvement. She even became engaged in a long conversation with someone who could quite possibly have been the killer of this group of young men. This man had handed himself into the police station in St

Charles, Missouri, telling them that he intended to be the next great and all time best Serial Killer. They cops laughed him out of the station. In fact, they even had to get a restraining order against him when he refused to quieten down.

Someone else took his threats and promises seriously however; the private detective hired by Chris Jenkins' family, after the police ruled that his drowning death had been an accident, even though he had very little water in his lungs, and a tracker dog indicated he had been bundled into a van. The detective, Chuck Loesch, had also come across this same man, when the man had been resident in Minneapolis, at the same time as Chris had disappeared. The fantasist was employed in a funeral parlour and incredibly disturbingly, he was a frequent visitor to a website called 'mandunderwater.com;' a pornographic website existing for those with a fetish for having intercourse under water.

Pat Brown, the criminologist, tracked him down on the website forum, and entered into a deceptive relationship with the man in an attempt to lure him into a confession, by posing as a young man who too had a fetish for such practises. Their correspondence became incredibly dark as they role-played together, with the man describing what he would like to do to the 'young man' who was in fact really Ms. Brown. He was a sadist, and what he described was chilling, highly disturbing, and fitted exactly the kind of person who would be capable of drowning young men. He specifically described killing her (posing as a young man) in very graphic detail in the fantasies he wrote to her. From her point of view, this man was capable of what he described to her. However, it wasn't taken seriously by the police according to her, or they denied knowing anything about it, and when he was put in prison for threatening his employer's family, another replica drowning occurred, only this time it couldn't have been him because he was incarcerated. So, perhaps he was just a fantasist?

There was also the case of Edward "Eddie" Lanphear, a regular employee at a paper mill in Wisconsin who had been employed there for a quarter of a century. No-one who worked with him would have ever expected him to have been arrested for the crimes he committed. He was described as a regular, quite guy. He wasn't someone who stood out. He lived outside of town in a small ranch with plenty of land. He was a separated father. He was 'a regular guy.' He liked the usual things; hunting, fishing, pool. He would go every few days down to a local bar, Johnny's, to play pool. He never drank when he was there; preferring soft drinks.

Perhaps now in hindsight, that was a good indication of something lurking inside him; there was nothing wrong with a man not drinking beer, but of course, it did make sure he always kept the clear head that he evidently needed.

It was an ordinary weekday evening in 1991, when a young man managed to escape from his ranch. He ran naked, bleeding, and still partially bound by the chains that had kept him prisoner in the basement of this ranch. He ran for his life, to the nearest neighbor's home and pounded on their door.

Later, what had actually happened to him would come to light. He'd been at the same bar, that prior weekend. He'd been drinking, and feeling very drunk, he'd managed to get himself outside and into his truck before passing out. When he woke, he was no longer in his own truck. When he opened his eyes he realized he was hanging by chains inside somewhere dark. His clothes had been taken off.

His captor was the quite tee-total pool player. He recognized him immediately from having seeing him in the bar many times. Then the quite man he recognized smashed his head with a metal pole, and sexually assaulted him, blindfolding him before he did so. After a couple of days of this, he somehow managed to free himself from the shackles and that was when he seized his chance and ran for his life. The police came to the neighbor's home immediately and went immediately to the ranch to arrest the mill worker. They also searched his property and to their shock they discovered someone else there; a young man who had vanished a few days before this. He too was being kept prisoner in the basement.

His version of what happened to him was a little different. He told the police that he'd been walking home from a firework display when the mill worker pulled over and offered him a ride home. The young man thought nothing of it and accepted the ride. However, as they neared the young man's address, the mill worker suddenly stopped his car and told the young man he was a cop. He handcuffed the young man; then knocked him out by hitting him with a large flashlight.

Just like the other young man who had later managed to flee, he too found himself chained up in a dark basement when he woke up. He too was beaten and sexually assaulted. The floor of the basement was covered with plastic sheeting. Like a scene from a horror movie, the mill worker had tied a piece of thin rope to the chains that bound him and attached the other end of the rope to a shotgun that was pointed directly at the young man. If the young man moved, the thin rope would tighten and pull the trigger.

While this man was not considered a suspect in the drowning deaths, it's a perfect example of just how easy it can be to overpower someone and abduct them.

The private detective mentioned earlier, Chuck Loesch, also discovered other possibilities while looking into the case of Chris Jenkins; things this time which pointed at a different possibility entirely. He heard about a group of individuals who collectively were calling themselves, 'The Dealers of Death.'

Jeramy Alford, a member of this so-called group, said that he had thrown Chris Jenkins off a bridge. He also said they had killed many of the other boys who 'drowned' too.

The private detective was not necessarily inclined to believe his story however; for a number of reasons. The bridge was covered by CCTV and there are no images depicting this crime. The forensic evidence also does not, in Loesch's opinion, corroborate this story. On the other hand, surveillance footage can of course be tampered with. The Police who worked on this case also did not support this confession; although they did say the victim's death was 'accidental,' until later when they changed it to homicide, so perhaps they are not the best to judge.

In terms of the forensics however, the young man's body did not have the kind of trauma that a fall like that would have produced, and he also was found still wearing slip on shoes; which is highly unlikely to be the case if he had been thrown. Interestingly however, it was months before he was found, and surely, as his Mother believes, the loose casual shoes he was wearing on the night of his disappearance, would not have still been on his feet, in waters with a flowing current. She *knows* he was murdered.

Jeramy Alford was said to have been attempting to recruit a vagabond group of misfits together, in order to create a gang that would take war to the streets. Unfortunately for him, he is now in prison for life, for a murder carried out in much more bloody way.

While the verdict on the existence and involvement of this gang appears to be very open, his sister has said, "Years ago when this stuff first came up, I believed he might of had something to do (with it) but as far as belonging to a gang, hell no. He's full of big talk but that's all it is, to make his friends think he's something."

On the other hand, an anonymous poster contradicts this statement; "I've been investigating these so called 'Dealers' for a few years now, and it seems their members are very secretive and range from petty thugs to fire-fighters, police officers, and CIA.

It seems they never truly reveal their identities to each another; instead, they use nicknames. They hold very secretive meetings, mostly in the heartland. It seems to follow some of the secret traditions of other Masonic orders. I followed this investigation to the top and high level members of the Government seem to acknowledge their existence somewhat but not on

record. If I was to estimate, I'd say at least two-thousand members, and it's nationwide."
Who is right? The sister or the investigator?

Milwaukee Magazine said back then, "After three months of research into these cases, a gang called the "Dealers of Death" claim involvement. Alford, told the FBI the gang had murdered at least 40 of the men. Another admitted gang member, called himself "Zmiley." According to the newspaper, some of the gang were apparently arrested for harbouring runaways and had branded one of them with a five-point star. Alford claimed they were part of a larger group; a political subdivision of another gang.

Local detective, Gary Sykes, believes they were behind street robberies to get money for drugs. As for their claim of murdering young men, "It's possible. They're capable of almost anything. They were just plain weird, and they have no compassion for human life."

What would be the connection then, between bright, athletic, high achieving college boys with promising futures and a dysfunctional assortment of drug takers and runaways, such as this kind of gang? Quite possibly the answer might lie in the people who recruit them. Easy to manipulate, easily turned to the dark side by their higher level puppet masters perhaps?

There are elements in these drowning cases which could lead to the theory that it's organised by an MK

Ultra-style project, and that the killers are doing this under instruction, either as part of their initiation, or as on-going work as 'assassins' for their Masters, who themselves are hidden well behind the smoke and mirrors. Researchers such as David McGowan, with his book 'Programmed to Kill,' clearly provided allegations of possible serial killer assassins, who have been created, manipulated, and programmed long before now.

If that were to be proven, it would indicate that the killers, or rather, those behind them, are both highly educated, and very intelligent. Some have suggested that the killers are therefore from an elite 'hunting' group; from elite Secret Societies such as 'the skull and bones' or a sub-strata of the illuminati.

They are certainly effective, because they are clean in their operation; their operation is slick, smooth and fast. It is never publicly messy, and it would appear, it also seldom fails, although later we will look at the possible cases of 'near-misses.'

Is it some kind of water boarding hazing initiation? Which goes too far, deliberately, to implicate those involved and serving as a perfect blackmail tool to use to keep them in the 'frat' or secret society for life? Or is it much more sophisticated than that?

On trying to get to an understanding of the possible perpetrators involved in this, one has to cover the wide range of possible theories that have sprung up over the years; many of which people have dedicated months of researching to. The most popular theories behind these sinister deaths, appear to be as follows; Air conditioning engineers who travel through colleges where A/C's are supplied. Native Americans who are seeking revenge, according to de-crypted word associations of places and names. Blacks targeting White college boys; but there have been deaths of men from other ethnicities. Alford's 'Dealers of Death cult.' Street gangs targeting frat boys. Specific frats carrying out the killings. Fans of the Insane Clown Posse. Spin-offs from the Son of Sam Cult or The Process Church. A sex trafficking ring. Snuff filmmakers. The Finders Organization; kidnapping and buying and selling, with CIA involvement/knowledge.

The biggest problem in trying to work out who could be doing it is that abductions take place sometimes on the same day in different states and even in different countries too. The same modus operandi, the same patterns; but in different places.

Professor L. Gilbertson has stated that they are like terrorists; operating out of different geographical areas, with cells based in each area. Terrorists, yet not of the ISIS type. Disturbingly, he says that young people are definitely in collusion; for the undisputable fact that so many times, the victims have been last seen in the company of unknown and unidentified young people, both men and women.

There are those that talk about these drowning deaths in terms of the numerology aspects to it, or clues in the names of the victims. They indicate and attempt to prove for example, that these victims are specifically chosen and that a combination of the letters in their names and the places they are either taken from, or found in, often spell out very intricate messages from the killers, which come from such sources as ancient texts, movies, art and literature. The suggested clues are complex and would require months and months of analysis to verify if there really is anything to this idea. Is it a possibility? Certainly, but it's hard to prove, and patterns, like statistics can be involuntarily skewed once objectivity is lost.

If it were to be proven however, it would indicate again that the killers are highly educated and very intelligent, or at least the ones giving the orders are.
Some have even spelt out words that appear to be taunting messages. 'COLD,' 'COP,' even 'Ha, Ho, Ha, Ha.'
In a wordpress blog no longer available, but quoted in various forums, they point out that the word NEMEC can be found from the first letters of the location in which several victims were found;
New London, Daniel Newville, (August 2002)
Eau Claire, Craig Burrows, (September 2002)

Minneapolis, Chris Jenkins, (October 2002)
Eau Claire, Michael Noll, (November 2002)
Collegeville, Josh Guimond, (November 2002)

Why is this possibly relevant? Well, in their opinion, this could apply to the name of an actor, Colin Nemec. He played the role of the true story of a boy called Steven Stayner. Coincidently, he was mentioned in my 'Mysterious things in the Woods' book, for the reason that after he was abducted as a child, his brother turned into a serial killer, who hunted, abducted and killed women in the Yosemite national park. In 1999, three female tourists had vanished from their rooms at the Cedar Lodge while in the park on a hiking trip. A few months later, they were found, brutally murdered in the woods.

Five months later, Joie Armstrong, 26, a naturalist at the Yosemite Institute, also went missing. Her truck was still parked in the driveway of her home at her cabin. Her body was found in the woods, not far from the cabin.

A park employee had noticed a car parked near her cabin on the night of her disappearance, and police issued an alert for the car. A few days later, police spotted the car parked up near Merced River Canyon. They came across a man wandering naked. He said his name was Cary Stayner and that he worked as a handyman at Cedar Lodge. After the encounter, investigators compared the car tyres to tyre tracks found at the crime scene, and they matched. The police found Stayner and arrested him. He confessed quickly and readily to all of the killings.

His own family history astonishingly revealed a disturbing crime perpetrated against his younger brother, and perhaps was what shaped him into becoming a serial killer. At the age of seven, his brother had disappeared without trace one afternoon in 1972, while walking home from school alone along the Yosemite Highway. Eight years later, Cary had heard an announcement on the radio that his brother had been found. It turned out that his brother had been abducted by a paedophile and former employee of the Yosemite Lodge, and kept prisoner for all of those years. Investigators wondered if Cary's homicidal behaviour had been caused perhaps by his own family's experience.

Colin Nemec played the role of the young brother in the subsequent movie. Nemec talks about Cary Stayner in the book The Yosemite Murders. Nemec is also mentioned in the book *I Know My First Name Is Steven*, which talks about the abduction. Is any of this at all in any way relevant? Or is it all just insane ramblings and attempts to form theories from random coincidences found in words and letters? In the case of the person who posted this NEMEC theory, they link it to the ATWA movement of Charles Manson, with ATWA being the acronym he created standing for Air, Trees,

Water, Animals and All the Way Alive; an ecological term the group designated to identify 'the forces of life which hold the balance of the earth.' With his small group of followers, prior to being imprisoned, it was Manson's attempt at eco living, though others say it was survivalist living.

It's this person's theory, explained on; themanyfacesofthezodiac.com/2013/04/07/charles-manson-link-to-smiley-face-murders/, that the college killings are a continuation of the Manson group, and that they are examples of mind-controlled, programmed individuals. "The Manson Family through ATWA has grown to a point now where I am sure even the FBI does not know the number."

His implication is that the group never went away with Manson's imprisonment; it carried on. And, now, they are leaving taunting messages; 'NEMEC' being a reference to a Serial Killer; Stayner. 'COP' perhaps attempting to implicate involvement of rogue cops; or, it's laughing at the cops for failing to stop these killings. 'COLD' of course, is the Water.

Then there is the study of Cryptocracy too. Both Michael A. Hoffman and James Shelby Downard believe that hidden connections and messages are revealed once this "twilight language" is understood. Wrote Hoffman, "The Wicker Man; the ancient symbol of ritual murder was resurrected into the group mind

consciousness with the Son of Sam murders, when they signed their Manifesto 'Wicked King Wicker."
'People learned to associate "him" with murder and terror. The alchemical processing of humans is then performed with the props of time and space; what happens ritually can 'bend' reality at places. That's what 'Wicker' means; it's the description of the end result of bending reality.'

Is this an example of what the alleged, still unknown, organized group of killers could be doing? Sending out messages, 'hidden in plain sight? Or is this all an absurd over-stretch to even try to see connections where there may be none? Very possibly. Micro-patterns appear, that can be misleading when viewed as a whole. Patterns can be found or formed if looking for them; but it doesn't mean they are necessarily the answer. Words, like statistics, can be manipulated innocently or willingly, by ignoring unrelated elements purposely, to make them show what you want them to, particularly as objectivity becomes lost in the pursuit of answers. It becomes easy to mislead oneself; as I may well be doing too.

Although tenuous and quite possibly wrong, this person's belief of an organised Manson group still existing, does tie in with David McGowan's position and his alleged research findings. He says that Mason's house was at one point in the same neighbourhood as Boy's Town, which was identified as an underground paedophile abduction ring during the Franklin Scandal (as referenced in 'Taken in the Woods' with regard to the Johnny Gosh abduction case).

According to McGowan, researcher Joel Norris makes the allegation that Manson was involved in a murder for hire ring and child pornography. He also alleges that Norris uncovered Manson's association with a satanic cult involved in sacrifice and murder. McGowan also states that another researcher, Ed Sanders, interviewed Manson's associates, and alleges that he was involved in the production of snuff movies. The theories go further however, with the claim that Manson was allegedly mind-controlled by the CIA through the use of drugs and mind programming. Actually, researchers such as McGowan implicated MK Ultra programs as being responsible for many of these 'programmed-to-kill' serial killing groups; Manson, Son of Sam, the Zodiac Killer.

The idea is then, that this 'group' are in fact 'mind controlled assassins' who hunt the selected and targeted male college victims. Interestingly, Manson once said, "Remember the pied piper; they never paid the piper so they kept losing their children. Well, you've lost six generations of children to me, because you won't pay me what you owe me." That could be viewed as a threat.

The story of the Pied Piper is that of the strangely dressed Trickster character who appeared in a town in the small rural town of Brunswick, in the county of Hamelin near Hanover in Germany. Though many probably remember this as a Fairy tale, in fact, documentation exists which show it actually happened. The year was 1284 A.D. and the event was recorded in the official town records, and later memorialised in a stained glass window of the Church there, dated to the year 300 A.D. The Pied Piper magically lured away all of the Town's children by playing them a tune on his flute. Before he did this, he used his magickal flute to lure all of the rats to the river's edge. He made them jump into the river and drown themselves. The fate of the children, is not known, but *somehow* they disappeared and were never found again.

At the time of the Manson trials, Ronald Hughes, the Defence Attorney who was acting for one of the Manson member's, Leslie van Houten, was found dead in a remote stream in Sespe Hot Springs near Ojai, Los Angeles. His death was ruled as 'accidental drowning,' yet he was in a position which was rather inaccessible. Manson was said to have threatened to kill him because he wouldn't let van Houten to testify to help get Manson off.

Manson was said by researchers to have been trying to create a plan to trigger the 'Helter Skelter' scenario; an apocalyptic war involving Revelations in the Bible. The group were said to have been trying to recruit a satanic army. Some believe it never stopped; only grew. On the other hand, it was said that the aim of this organization at the time of the 'Helter Skelter' plan, was supposed to be to cause a war by create racial tension, but of course, the young men in this case are mainly Caucasian, so perhaps pointing in this direction is way off mark; unless their deaths were being attributed to groups of other ethnicity, which it doesn't seem to be.

Interestingly, there was a time during the Irish Troubles when British Intelligence created a satanic panic over the killing of a young boy by allowing it to look like he had been killed for satanic ritual purposes, as a means of creating fear in the community. It wasn't satanic, but they allowed that rumor to circulate and it was used for Psy-ops. The satanic angle never really existed.

Researcher Ed Sander believes that he discovered Manson and his cohorts were being controlled by the CIA, through the use of drugs and mind programming. The idea was that they were being mind controlled into becoming 'assassins' of sort. On the other hand, how credible is this really? Yes, evidence was potentially found to prove it could have been happening back then; but still continuing?

Well, according to someone who tracked these type of organizations for decades, Ret'd NYPD James Rothstein, who is an expert in human trafficking, he fully believes that this organization, as well as others such as The Process Church, never went away; that they still exist in some underground form. Of this, Rothstein has experience of, and he may know more about this than most. Now retired from NYPD, the ex-detective is Mayor of St Martin's, Minnesota, and has talked extensively of his investigations into human trafficking and child abduction, and pointing to elite paedophile rings being at the top of the chain; shadowy groups concealed, cloaked and hidden, and held together by secret blood oaths.

Rothstein worked closely on not only Human trafficking, but satanic cults and all manner of underground crime from vice to blackmail and drugs dealing. He talks of the Process Church, which began in England, transported to New Orleans and then ended up in the Bronx in New York. Off-shoots of it grew, all of which knew each other in an underground movement. He says that in the late 1970's when they realised that the cops were moving in on the Son of Sam killers in New York City, they uprooted once more and headed Westwards. He is of the firm belief that these 'smiley face killers' are the handiwork of an organization such as the Process Church or an offshoot of such. "They are all connected," he says, "and they are all aware of what each off shoot is doing."

Of course, the Process Church was associated with Charles Manson too. Then again, many have pointed out that the Process Church was also said to have been born from the Scientology Church, and Rothstein alleges that now, the Process Church resides in the Western side of the States too.

Rothstein says he has tracked this group for over forty years. When he spoke with Ret'd Detective Gannon, the original investigator of these drownings, he says he told him "The geographic designation of the 'Church' matches very closely that of the early killing sites, in the mid-west areas of Wisconsin and Minnesota."

Is he right? Or is it simply a case of the most obvious suspects? Isn't it the easiest answer to point to a group and say it's 'the satanists'? In fact, were these groups even really involved in any of the earlier killings like the Son of Sam? And Zodiac? It's a topic that has been hotly debated for decades now, and there are really no clear answers at all.

If he were right, what about all the deaths that have happened in other States, on the same nights? Surely an organization like that would not stretch across the entire country?

What's interesting to note is that Rothstein comments on The Finders organisation too, "the Finders organization; it's so far from the truth, what you read about it now. It was an operation; a lot of it was for Intel. gathering. A bus load of kids were stopped in a van driven by men. The men said they were being taken to a special school. The children were nearly naked, and filthy dirty. The men in the van were traced back to a warehouse, run by the CIA," says Rothstein.

"The Franklin cover-up of Boystown, (the town Manson once resided in) was given to me in a report. I'm very familiar with what did happen and what didn't. Johnny Gosh I've done a lot of work on."

Twelve year old Johnny Gosch was abducted while on his Newspaper delivery round in Des Moines, Iowa, in September 1982. His Mother claimed an abduction 'ring' which was part of the earlier established MK-Ultra program, was behind it, even giving testimony in Court of what she believed to be a Nationwide Satanic ring of paedophiles. Talking on the Opperman Report radio show, he says, "When he was kidnapped; he was the first of 4 boys kidnapped," says Rothstein. "*Someone* had a fetish for paper boys. The 5th escaped. Jacob Wetterling was one of the boys." Jacob Wetterling was kidnapped from his Minnesota neighborhood in 1989. Rothstein's sources say it happened often, for money.

"Kids were being grabbed to satisfy the twisted depravity of very powerful individuals who have the money," he says. "You could order one of these kids; it was $2,500 to $3,000 up front in some cases...these people would hand that money out like it was candy. I can tell you without a doubt that there was a man 'the agency' assigned to investigate this because they were afraid it would go back to other cases. There were

1,500 victims and 834 children fell into the same 'category.'"

He is implying here, that all of the boys were used for a specific purpose. He doesn't say how they were used, but clearly it was something truly horrific. He says both he and Johnny's mother were sent photos of her kidnapped son. They were pornographic in nature. "They are the epitome (the perfect classic example) of these cases hitting the heartland," he says.

Of MK Ultra, he says, "We saw all these unimaginable experiments and victims; we would take them to mental wards. This all worked together and that's how they did it. We caught a man who was working in the Intel field who was compromising certain people. He killed two fourteen year olds. Years later we were able to get a subpoena to get him to testify to the crime."

"By the time we got to his office to question him they had it under "national security;" we never got to question the guy. We tracked MK Ultra, arresting a woman attached to it. We took it to the very top. It all blended together, and that's why they had a lot of resources." He means here; it was 'funded.'

His implication then is that it's probably most likely that these 'drowning' deaths' are the result of a very organized, high level group who are happy to let it appear that those behind it are a bunch of Satanists, or that they actively encourage it and are involved in it.

Perhaps its merely camouflaged to look like Satanism; with the graffiti of crowns and horns being left, and a mind control trick used to lure "useful idiots and patsies" to carry out these sacrifices; with those doing it not realising they are merely being used by those higher up in the hierarchy as a 'front' to disguise who is really behind it. But if so, again, what is their motive?

Could it really be true that children and adults are abducted for sacrificial satanic cults? Or, do they become victims of a powerful underground elite, operating from the highest levels down? Is this in any way plausible or just crazy and unfounded speculation? Well, Rothstein himself says he has experience of it existing. Yet, what exactly is the reason behind this?

What has to be considered is that these are 'clean,' sleek, and successful kills; almost silent in operation. What does that tell us about those who may really be doing it? That doesn't sound like a group of Satanists, but it also offers no obvious reason as to why a 'Government/Military organization would be doing this either.

Could it be really part of an ongoing MK Ultra? When investigated, the program had consisted of 149 'subprojects' which the Agency had contracted out to various *Universities* and institutions. Is it still going strong?

There's also the case of the missing boy Daniel Nolan, in which the controversial numerologist and esoteric expert Ellis C Taylor is explicit in his belief that not only does satanic ritual of the elite take place on energy ley lines of power, but that this is inextricably linked to the disappearance and deaths of missing children in the United Kingdom.

He claims to have identified 'patterns' in these 'abductions and murders' of children and teenagers over the last few decades which strongly tie in with both important occult dates, numerology, and Ley lines. The path of travel in these abduction and murder cases, he believes, are via Ley lines which intersect ancient places of powerful black energy. His implication is that occult ritual sacrifice is being conducted to harness the black energy.

He ties the location of where they go missing and the location in which they are found to these lines and links them directly through lines that run through Satanic places of worship, ancient sites, and indeed even claims that these lines directly lead to places that clearly indicate exactly who is involved in these ritual murders. Daniel Nolan was a teenage boy who disappeared after night fishing with his friends in January 2002.

They'd been fishing off the Hamble waterfront, near Southampton, on the coast of south of England. Fourteen year old Daniel had fished many times before.

His main hobbies were fishing, canoeing and swimming. He was a member of the Sea Scouts. Sniffer dogs could pick up no scent of him. Five teams of police divers and two army sonar units could also detect no trace of him. Almost a year later, a lady was walking her dog in a scenic bay called Chapman's Pool near Swanage, in Dorset. An entirely different county and over forty miles away. She stumbled across a shocking sight. It was a human foot still in its shoe, washed up onto the beach.

After DNA forensic analysis found that it was part of Daniel's body, tidal experts were brought in to try to explain how the foot, still in the trainer and sock, had managed to travel 40 miles in the sea. The area in which this part of his body was discovered, though accessible to those local to the area with knowledge and experience of climbing down into the bay, is not an easy nor simple path to take. It can be accessed though, and it can also be accessed by simply dropping anchor further out of the bay.

David Ike claims that Ley-lines are used by determined occultists, who seek to use these lines for their own agenda. These Luciferians he says, manipulate this strong energy field into a greater form of density. 'While we see everything as *physical*, the *energy* construct is the place where everything originates; that's why the Elite spend so much effort manipulating this energy; because if you want to affect all the fish, you need to affect this *energy* sea in which we all live. This repetition of ritual practice has over time left strong impressions. Occultists work to keep this energy grid suppressed at these critical intersections, by ritual. Satanic rituals are performed on these lines. Water itself an excellent collector of energy.'

Arrangements are made, he says, to manipulate and 'negatively charge' these energy flows. If this sounds a little over-dramatic, perhaps we should consider researcher David Gowan, said to be an authority on Ley Lines. He believes, 'The world's ley lines have been used by secret societies for thousands of years.' He believes that they who harness this ancient power are now able to control humanity by manipulating this energy system to meet their own agendas. Cowan believes both white and black energy spirals emanate from the earth in certain places, with natural white energy spiralling upward, but black energy spirals the other way and is extremely harmful.

These can be naturally occurring, or deliberately blackened energy, made so by occultists. He cites cases of poltergeists and demonic possessions that he's investigated as being caused by entities manifesting through this black energy, able to enter our dimension.

His years of studying these ley line routes as natural sources of power which were once used as a tool for healing, has led him to discover that there has been a deliberate occult manipulation of them, turning them into blackened energy lines which are used instead for evil purposes by garnering and enhancing their power to serve a cabal of dark worshippers. In his opinion, some of these ley lines have been *man-made* and set with deliberate intention on a certain path to negatively influence locations, including the ancient stones across the world. He believes that as the ley lines travel, they pass through water and lakes and through 'crevices' or 'cavities' in the land. They can be 'captured' in these cavities and the energy harnessed there.

Water or 'cavities' can pull the energy into it from the ley line, trapping it and enhancing it. From this can be made the black energy spirals. Just as the natural 'white' energy of the ley lines are positive and healing, so the black man-made occult ones are negative and destructive to those who encounter them. If energy grids of pure black energy were created and criss-cross a region, it's reasoned that negative actions and behaviors could be caused. And so the theory goes that these negative energy grids have been put in place by the destructive elite who wish to subliminally control the population. It's claimed that his book was immediately mysteriously withdrawn from publication on the day it was released. Believers in his work and conspiracy theorists alike have speculated, was this man getting too close to exposing the truth about the secret elite societies harnessing and manipulating the ancient occult powers of these energy fields?

Was his book instantly pulled by pressure from those who control the puppet strings, in order to keep this ancient occult knowledge to themselves? they asked.

Some even claim to have charted a straight ley line running from Stonehenge to Sandy Hook school and state that satanic sacrifice ritual was the motive of the massacre at Connecticut. One is Fernando Tognola, of 9/11 Truth.ch, who charted them on his site. Explanations of the precise geographic charting and numeric calculations required to chart this oneself are difficult to understand for a layman, such as the Author of this book, but it makes for some compelling reading attempting to understand it. Suffice it to say, there are many who are able to understand the intricacies of charting and make claim to its accuracy, and they cite it as proof that the secret sects who seek to control society through a demonic agenda are always carrying out such atrocities in attempts to harness and grow the power they feed through such rituals.

As Tesla himself said, 'to find the secrets think in terms of energy, frequency and vibration.' All matter is now known to be differing vibrational energy, whether animate or inanimate. It doesn't matter if we don't accept that the earth's floor is formed of these dynamic energy grids, but perhaps we should at least be aware of those do and are, as has been suggested, seeking to use them to their distinct advantage against us?

As David Cowan believes, 'Those who knew of the ancient secrets of the earth's natural energy systems are now able to control humanity by the manipulation of these natural features in the energy grid for their own sinister purposes.'

What type of organized group could really be doing this? A group of travelling and highly organised serial killers? A weird fraternity-related cult? A fanatical religious or satanic group? An MK Ultra-style set up? An elite faction at the lower echelons of the illuminati? And above all, what is their purpose?

I'm afraid it's really not that simple.....as will later be discussed...

Chapter 8:
The Possibilities Continue

Is the water just simply being used in an attempt to try to wash away some of the evidence? Or, is there some kind of symbolism involved with the water? Is some kind of elite group conducting ancient rituals to further enhance their desire for power? Is there any possibility of these deaths being ritual sacrifices, based on the ancient beliefs that the victim's life-force energy can be passed to the occult murderer(s) at the moment of the victim's death, supposedly giving them enhanced 'power' through their consciousness?
In alchemical ritual, a solid substance is said to be 'disolved' in water in a 'slow and silent operation.'

When writing 'Something in the Woods,' I came across the case of the Jamison family. It made me wonder about ritual water death, as will be explained. There was a very strong possibility that the Jamison's too had ended up dead in water. The Jamison family; husband, wife and their six year old daughter had headed out to the Latimer Mountains of Oklahoma, October 8th 2009, to view some land they were considering buying. After family members realised they had not returned, an enormous search party was organised with hundreds of volunteers, troopers from the Oklahoma Highway Patrol and, agents from the FBI. They combed the area on foot, on ATV's, and on horses, but they found nothing;

even the multiple teams of tracker dogs that had been used.

Then, a few days later their truck was discovered by hunters. It was locked and inside it the family's dog was close to death. Investigators discovered the family's cell phones and a very large amount of cash; there were no tracks however to lead them to where the family could have gone. The 31-year-old Sheriff, a former U.S. Army Ranger, said his mind was consumed by questions and theories."Throughout this whole process I've found myself going back and forth as to what might have happened," Israel Beauchamp said, "I'm at my wit's end. I asked for all the help I could get. FBI agents; private investigators who contacted me."

If it had been straight forward foul play, surely the perpetrators would have stolen the money; there was over $30,000 in cash in the vehicle? A man who lived a quarter mile from where the pickup was found was the last known person to see them. He was questioned, ruled out as having had any involvement and he said that he had seen no-one else in the vicinity. Local rumors led some to wonder if it was it a drug deal gone bad. Were they drug users? Others have wondered were they in the process of turning state's evidence against drug dealers? Was it simply a criminal case; or was there something much deeper to this? As people in the area speculated and tried to understand what had happened to the family, an edition of *The Oklahoman* headlined the story. The mother of Sherilyn Jamison was telling the Newspaper that her daughter "was on a cult's hit list."

According to Oklahoma's *Red Dirt News*, husband Bobby had allegedly been reading a "Satanic Bible" and had asked a Church Minister how he could obtain "special bullets" that would enable him to kill the demons that were terrorizing the family. Security camera footage recorded at their home, installed by the family due to their concerns of the alleged spiritual attacks they were complaining of. It shows both adults walking around at times in a trance-like states and disorientation prior to their departure.

Approximately a month before the disappearance of the family, local Pastor Carol Daniels was found horrifically murdered in her Church nearby. The local D.A. Mr Burns said of the crime scene that it was "the most horrific he'd ever seen," but he wouldn't go into details as to why. Her mutilated body though was found behind the Church Altar in a crucifix pose, obviously suggesting a link to Satanic ritual. Then in November 2013, the bodies of two adults and a child were found by a deer hunter about four miles from their truck. It was believed to be the skeletal remnants of the family. This was odd because the Jamison father could not walk more than a few metres without experiencing severe pain, and Sherylin had chronic pain in her neck and shoulder. Both were on disability, yet they were found on the opposite side of the low mountain area where they'd left their truck.

Their 'abduction' has echoes of eerily similar unexplained missing person's cases that have been documented over the last few decades; the 'abduction' takes place in a remote wilderness area with dense or difficult terrain. The 'abductors' one assumes, must have had the ability to not only control and transport these people from their truck through rugged terrain; they also left no other vehicle tracks, nor footprints, nor scent.

While the Jamison's fate may simply be a case of human intervention, *Reddirt news* make a point of the synchronicity that both the area where their bodies were found, and the site of the Church where the pastor was murdered fall on the 'Occult line of tragedy;' on the 33rd parallel north.

Occultists see the number 33 as containing the highest of sacred power. Occult scholars and conspiracists claim that the Illuminati and the 'power elite' have staged murders on or near the 33rd parallel north throughout history. In Occult belief, sacrificial rites enacted at the 33rd parallel have far more power than any other geographical locations. 33 is the satanic number of completion, and holds the power of transmutation.

According to expert Occultists and conspiracists alike, including the late occult researcher John Downard, it's the 'kill number;' and the murders carried out are for a ritual called the 'Killing of the Kings' where the life-force is believed to be passed from the victim at the point of death to those carrying out the ritual.

Curiously, there was a similar case in 2013, in Eufaula, the Jamison's home town. Thirty year old Native American Tommy Eastep vanished on his return journey after spending a July 4th weekend trip there visiting his family. His truck was found abandoned on September 29th, in a rural area north of Holdenville; his keys, credit card and driver's license locked inside. According to his older brother Clint, talking on blog talk radio, it was a good four miles off the main highway on a county road more like a cattle road. He says, "It was parked as deep as you could go. It probably stopped because there was overhanging tree and the truck couldn't go any further. There's a lake nearby, lots of small ponds around, and a large heavily-wooded area to the south and west.

Clint says, "He was a family man. He had kids. He wasn't in any type of turmoil, you know, that he walked off without his license, his debit card, his keys, his vehicle, and his belongings. He did not walk away."

Despite tracker dogs searching throughout the area his truck was found in, no trace of him has been found still. There is no suggestion here of occult intervention, although again his abandoned vehicle was found at a cross roads on the same symbolic degree of latitude.

Returning to the Jamison family, some sources, including Discovery TV, state that the tracker dogs *did* trace their scent, to a water tank near where their vehicle was found. This was an indication that their bodies had likely been placed inside the water tank, but when it was emptied they were not found inside. Were they killed in the water? They were found almost three miles away with no tracks and both were partially disabled and unlikely to have walked that far voluntarily. Despite the search radius being extensive, they were not found during all the searches. Where had they been? Were they kept in the water tower? Or were they kept somewhere else?

Interestingly, adding to the idea of a water ritual theory, as discussed in detail in "Something in the Woods," was the case of Elisa Lam, whose death features a water tower too; only in her case, she was found dead in the water, unlike the Jamison family, who it can be suggested had perhaps been placed in the water, and then removed. This time the water tank was on the rooftop of a hotel. Partly captured on film is the shocking and mysterious death of Elisa Lam. In June 2013, investigators ruled her death as 'accidental,' with 'bi-polar' listed as significant. So, perhaps she died as a result of suffering from a particularly bad onset of her condition. Several important questions however have failed to be answered. One of which is, why would she climb over fifteen feet up into a water tower on the roof of a hotel to get inside it? Another would be; what exactly was happening to her in the security footage of her in the hotel lift prior to her disappearance?

The twenty one year old Canadian student was staying at a cheap hotel in downtown Los Angeles while travelling on her own, taking some time out from college. She was found naked in the water tower, having been dead for two weeks. She was last seen on the CCTV camera in the lift, sometime before she ended up in the water tower. The parts in between are a mystery, but so too is what's happening to her in the lift.

Able to be watched on YouTube, the footage is difficult to comprehend and very eerie. There is something very wrong going on. She is seen entering the lift and pressing lots of the buttons quickly, then peeking out of the open door several times while she waits for the lift to close. It's almost as though she is fearful that someone is after her. Looking along the corridors, she waits as the lift door fail to close. Becoming increasingly distressed, she's seen making odd gestures with her hands, stepping out of the lift and hiding in the corridor, seeming to be terrified yet not fleeing the scene. Is her imagination playing tricks with her? Is her killer there out of sight of the CCTV, but lurking within inches of her, waiting to abduct her? Is there something otherworldly about what is happening? Some people studying the tape have implied there are strange shadows and movement seen inside the lift; shadowy movement, and even face-type forms appearing on the walls of the lift.

Is this merely poor video quality and over-active imaginations, or was there something unidentifiable and supernatural manifesting in the lift with her? At one point, she is seen waving her hands around in front of her, as though trying to feel for what is touching her and talking to her, that she cannot see. When she realizes there is an intangible, invisible entity inside the lift with her, her horror grows and she becomes terrified, wrenching her hands together and bending her knees in fright, trying to maintain her grip on sanity when she does not understand what is happening to her.

Her behaviour is one of disorientation, fear, helplessness and shock. Some will say she was on drugs but none were found in her system. Others will say she was having a break-down but the tragic case has fascinated many and there are some incredible theories going around. Some strongly believe she was about to be attacked by something unseen. Others feel her strange behaviour points to demonic possession and that she was clearly hearing voices. There's also the theory that she may have she died in an occult ritual; that she was used as a sacrifice, hinting at her name and the likeness to Aleister Crowley's poem 'Jephtha,' written when he was staying at the Cecil Hotel in London, the same name as the hotel in which she died.

They have pointed out that the poem has the line 'Be seen in some high lonely Tower.' In the poem, 'Jeptha' was a judge in the *Pseudo-Philo* works, (an ancient biblical text) who offered his daughter as a willing sacrifice. The girl is called Seila; an anagram of Elisa. A coincidence perhaps? A conspiracy too far? Others have speculated that she had been wanting to commit suicide. The hotel itself has an unsettling history of murder which may perhaps have left some kind of supernatural imprint on the building; its malevolent aura urging people on to commit acts of murder there. There are records of two serial killers having lived at the hotel. The hotel has also had an unusually high number of suicides. However, there were far easier ways to do it. Was it even possible to get into the water tank of her own accord? There was no ladder there.

Is this all hysteria and speculation? Was she simply trying to get an old temperamental lift to move, by getting in and out of it and pressing all of the buttons, trying to see which one would get it moving? But why does the security tape look like she's talking to someone who is not visible and reaching her hands out and grasping the empty space in front of her as though trying to feel for something invisible that is right in front of her but that she cannot see. What is making her so distressed and confused?

Adding to the mystery is Dr Douglas James Cottrell, PhD. A highly regarded Canadian medical intuitive who claims he, like his predecessor Edgar Cayce, can access the Akashic Hall of Records. Through this he has given thousands of personal readings to people regarding their health problems, accessing their undiagnosed illnesses through a form of 'remote viewing.' A former skeptic himself, it was when his child was born with a serious illness that he sought help with the diagnosis and through this journey met others like him who could help heal people. He undergoes deep meditative states to look into the past and the future, and is believed to be able to make accurate predictions and see what happened in past events. In one session available on YouTube, he relates what he 'sees' as having happened to Elisa Lam in the lift and up on the roof of the hotel. He alleges that she was hearing voices in her head; but this was not from a psychotic breakdown, and it was not a demon.

The voices were being 'beamed' into her head. They were calling her name, beckoning her; she was looking for the source of the voices and could not understand why she couldn't see the person or people around her when the voices were so close. They were high pitched and uncomfortable, they were causing her distress, disorientation and fear. She was obeying the voices, going to where they were beckoning her so that she could find them. They led her to the water tower, says Dr Cottrell. They led her to her death and when she got to the roof he alleges, in his meditative trance state, there were pains in her head as though someone was pointing a laser beam at her head. Self-destructive thoughts were being given to her through the sound waves being sent through this 'laser' he claims. Chillingly he says he can see a dark figure on the roof; cloaked in dark shiny clothing, a shadowed figure with its head covered by a balaclava or hood. He thinks it's a man but he also says it's possible it's a *discarnate* entity.

As Max Heindel says, in *The Rosicrucian Cosmo-Conception*, 'The first step in Occultism is the study of the *Invisible* Worlds; non-existent and incomprehensible, because we lack the sight to perceive them. The mysterious force which causes phenomena remains invisible to us, but if with methods our higher senses are awakened, we are able to behold the Worlds hidden. The reality of these higher Worlds and the objects in them appear as 'mirages' or even less substantial, yet in truth they are much more real and more indestructible than the objects in the 'physical' world.'

Others point to her online activity. Was a tweet allegedly sent from Elisa's twitter account really hers?

There's the claim that from her twitter account, before her stay in the hotel, she tweeted a post about a Canadian company being given funding from the US for developing a 'quantum stealth' type of camouflage for soldiers that makes them invisible. The gear blends light around the wearer/ or an object, to create the illusion of invisibility. In that respect, a soldier, or anyone using it, can render themselves invisible to everyone else. Has the development of cloaking technology created invisible predators that the unsuspecting person is powerless to see coming? Are people being silently snatched by something human but invisible?

These wild ideas and speculations could all be a range of conspiracy theories that have gone way too far; but perhaps not. What's interesting to note here is that her autopsy report, which lists her death as "accident," also says that although toxicology was done, "quantitation in the blood was not performed due to limited sample available."

What this is saying is that Elisa Lam was missing most of her blood. How did she come to be dead in the water, with no signs of foul play, and yet having apparently been exsanguinated? This was the case for one of the early 'drowning' college men deaths; Jeff Geesy did not drown in the river in which he was found. He died hours before that, even though he had been missing for more than 40 days. He had been hanging upside down before he was killed, then transported to the site of the water, and placed into the water.

Of course, in the case of the drowning young men, it is happening everywhere, not just in water towers. This drowning ritual theory of the Jamisons' deaths could perhaps tie-in with the ritual motive however when looking at some of the other similar cases; in particular in La Crosse, Wisconsin, as will be explained shortly. Strangely, it was a former Medical Examiner there himself who took to an unorthodox method in an attempt to try to discover the truth. Now retired, Neil Sanders believes there is much more to these deaths than accidental drownings. So much so that he made the documentary 'The Hidden Truth,' enlisting film producer Scott Markus, who worked on the 'Dark Knight' Batman movie and other Hollywood blockbusters. Everyone worked for free on the film, believing it to be an important cause and a film that needed to be made. Sanders brought in a team of paranormal investigators to assist in creating the documentary; having seen the evidence of the drowning cases and finding no answers there he prepared to consider less conventional alternatives in order to try to solve the mystery.

"All normal angles had previously been investigated when looking into these cases; except for one, and that's the paranormal," he tells journalist Ken

Luchterhand. "Paranormal just means *other than normal*." However, he does feel he was prompted to make the film by a couple of very unusual incidents. "I had a visit from my dad and he told me I needed to investigate the deaths, then just a few days later my brother came and told me to do the same thing; my brother died four years ago, my dad died two years ago."

Sanders took their advice and brought Wisconsin Paranormal Investigators (WPI) on board. He wanted to know if they could find any supernatural reasons for the deaths. He also spoke to elders of the Ho-Chunk Native American tribe. While filming them talking about water spirits, all of the microphones failed. None of the audio could be captured. Then it happened again when they took a boat out onto the river one night. They were trying to capture EVP, but all of the full charged batteries went dead. They had to abandon and return the next night. This time they did manage to make recordings, although they didn't think they'd captured anything. However when they listened to the recording later that night, they said they could hear voices on it and screams. The completion of the documentary left the makers of it just as baffled as before. Nothing provided anything like a conclusive lead or answer. Then another college boy drowned.

In July 2014 another young man, Shalim, was found dead in the river. There were no signs of foul play. He'd disappeared after walking away from the Marina, telling friends there that he was walking home. He was found upstream; not downstream, which is perhaps a little unusual. He was a bartender and not one to drink while at work, and he had been an altar boy at Church. Which leads on to one aspect of the possible theories about this mystery, particularly in the La Cross area.

A private investigator hired by one victim's family, the Jenkins', used tracker dogs that allegedly led them to an Abbey there, where the scent then stopped. The odd thing was, their son went to a different University altogether, not Collegeville St John's University and he had never been in that area. His scent was found along with another boy, who attended University very close-by. This boy, Joshua Guimond, has never been found.

Joshua Guimond went missing from the grounds of the Benedictine St Johns Abbeville and University Collegeville, Minnesota, on the night of November the 9th, nine days after Jenkins went missing. The dog tracked toward the lake behind the Abbey, but the boy's body was not found in the water there.
He was last seen leaving a dorm room just a couple of minutes walk from his own dorm, but he never reached his own. He didn't have his glasses on, he had no coat on, and no car. What's strange is that the dog also picked up another boy's scent, a boy called Chris Jenkins, a student at the University of Minnesota, who had been found dead in the Mississippi River with his

arms folded across his body, in a manner which is wholly inconsistent with drowning. There was GHB in his system. He too had been 'kicked out' of a bar. He had never been to this college campus. His mother has said, "The evil is rampant, deep and widespread. He was abducted, driven around for hours and tortured; then taken to the river and killed. Then, his body was "positioned" and taken to a different part of the river and left."

This Abbey has what can only be described as a shocking history, and a history that spills over to the present. On the Abbey's website is a public apology to all who have been abused by Priests residing there, and it lists eighteen names, including nine monks still living there, described as being 'under a supervised plan.' More than 250 allegations of sexual and other misconduct have been alleged to date.

Pat Marker, who says that he was abused while a student there, goes further. He claims there are over two hundred victims of abuse, and more than fifty monks involved, as well as men associated with the college but not actual monks. This has led some interested in the deaths of the young men to look more deeply into a religious motive. The combination of some claims (refuted by the original team who investigated it) that religious jewellery was missing, the tracker dogs tracing the scent of two of the boys to the college, and the allegations of sexual abuse of boys, creates a potent theory; a theory taken further in an astonishing twist by some people on forums. In particular, what intriguingly appears to be someone very highly schooled in alchemy has spent a significant amount of time and effort looking into this mystery, with some compelling conclusions;

'The Killers are committing Human Sacrifice as part of an alchemical ritual; using the human body for occult development, and transmuting the matter of their body into ever purer forms of energy.' In particular 'the writer' believes they have identified the specific ritual. 'It's called "the killing of the Little King," by drowning.' They claim to have also uncovered that Monks at the Abbey were posting on a very specialized alchemy forum. 'Here they discuss this drowning ritual; it's a representation of the dissolution of matter and identity, and the first stage of the 'Great ritual'; "the Purification," and the alchemist will (later) bathe in a tincture taken from the dead man.'

Could this be the key? Or, is this being taken too literally? Is it rather, a metaphor?

In Sir James George Frazer's 'The Golden Bough; *A Study in Magic and Religion*,' written in 1922, he discusses this human sacrifice of the 'dying God,' and 'the scapegoat.' 'The man God must be killed as soon as he shows symptoms that his powers are beginning to fail and his soul must be transferred to a vigorous successor. If the man-God dies a natural death it means that his soul has departed voluntarily or had been extracted or detained by a demon or sorcerer; whereas by slaying him, his worshippers could make sure of catching his soul and transferring it to a suitable successor. The mystic kings of Cambodia are not allowed to die a natural death."

Of course, Fraser was studying the ancient customs of tribes in places such as Africa and Egypt. Surely this bears no relevance to today, or the West? Is this what's really going on? As will later be explained, it's not quite as fantastical as it sounds. There are some who are convinced that this is very much going on, and is a deadly reality. In terms of it pointing to the Abbey at that Campus; it's highly unlikely it's them. In fact, investigation into the person posting this information about the monks, rather strangely led to claims by others that this person themselves possibly had their own rather odd "manifesto", and the thoughts then arise that perhaps this person was possibly using the Abbey as a kind of red herring to draw any possible attention away from the real perpetrators?

This is a theme which has recurred as I have attempted over the years to get to the facts about what is really happening. The term 'rabbit hole' certainly applies here.

Interestingly, a man called Jamie Connolly wrote to me recently, "The murders may be connected to the Cistercians. The Old Cistercians founded their Churches, Abbeys, and Monasteries upon rivers, streams, lakes, brooks... they have a Big connection to water... And Old St Bernard who helped form the Knights Templar was a Cistercian."

It could be a real stretch, but though St John's Abbeville is described as 'Benedictine,' the actual differences between religious orders are said to be fewer than the layman might initially expect. For someone who is attempting to discern the difference, apparently this may come as a surprise. Again, it's not here to say that the Abbey is responsible at all; it's to say that it could be any Monastery or Order, who is either Cistercian or Benedictine quite possibly.

Interestingly, the Knights Templar are known in history as the warrior monks who were tortured and made to confess to worshipping Baphomet, a daemon God, but what is not as commonly known is the kinship the Templars shared with the Cistercians, the true and original monks.

"The very rule of the Templar order held this monastic institution in highest regard, and there is no doubt of the ventures between the two. If a Knight was expelled from the order, he was required to seek shelter in a Cistercian monastery," says Stephen A. Dafoe.

When the Knights were tortured at their inquisition, some admitted to worshipping Baphomet. However, it has to be pointed out here however that given mediaeval torture methods, surely anyone would confess to anything to try to stop the sheer agony of their torture. However, the theory goes that not only did the Knights Templar work in some kind of allegiance with the Cistercian Monks, but so too were they enmeshed in Secret Societies, and while enmeshed in them, they were serving a Master that was not God, in a secret and hidden doctrine.

Eliphas Levi once wrote, "The Templars went so far as to recognize the pantheistic symbolism of the grand masters of Black Magic."
Occult writer Tracy Twyman refers to the sex rites, which many of the knights confessed to, involving homosexuality, paedophilia and bestiality, and of course, human sacrifice of children during their ceremonies, supposedly. She quotes Orientalist scholar Joseph Baron von Hammer-Purgstall, who wrote of Baphomet in the early 1900's; "Baphomet" came from the Greek "Baphe meteos, meaning '*tincture' (or baptism) and the personification of Divine wisdom; the mother of the Demiurge.*'

The relevance of the word 'Demiurge' is something which will become much more apparent a little later in this book.

Note the use of the word too 'baptism' or 'tincture.' Perhaps there really are those who believe then that these ritual 'baptisms' are necessary? Of course, here perhaps 'Baptism by Torture' should also perhaps be considered. According to scholar William Schweiker, of the University of Chicago, 'Practices similar to waterboarding developed as a way to torture heretics;

protestants as wells as Jews and witches. The use of this torture was meant to stem the movement and bring 'salvation' to these heretics.'

'It had been done at least since the time of St Augustine, (stemming from the Council of Nicea) and it could be justified as an act of mercy, even when done in lethal form, it was meant as an act to keep the sinner from continuing to sin, and the choice offered in this 'baptism by torture' was either repentance of heresy or death by drowning.` King Ferdinand called drowning the 'Third Baptism' and a suitable response to Anabaptists. It held the grotesque belief that the water death, or threat of, could deliver the heretic from his sins. The victim was forced to ingest water poured into a cloth stuffed in their mouth, to give the sensation of drowning. Torture by water drew its power from the theological beliefs and principles about repentance and salvation."

Chapter 9:
Near Misses

Are there any potential victims? Ones that have managed, somehow, to survive? Is there anything that they can tell us? Are there any unsuccessful attempts? Why are there never any witnesses? Or are there?

Earlier, we had the case of Cullen, whose Mother spoke out about her son being found in the Emergency Room of their local hospital, after finding himself desperately dragging his way out of the Mississippi, with no recollection as to how he had got in there.

Nancy from Spirit Lake, in Dickinson County, Iowa, writes, 'Last Friday night, in Spirit Lake, a young man was stopped and asked for directions. As he approached the car he was grabbed from behind. His hands were tied and he was put in the back seat. The two men then drove him to a remote lake. They untied his hands and held him under water until they thought he was dead. He's a swimmer; and he has a record for holding his breath under water. He faked that he'd drowned. He remained in the water terrified, for what felt like hours, and then found his way to a near-by house and the police were called. This young man is related to my sister. When she called the FBI they told her they didn't see a link!'

How do we really know if this is true? We don't, but it's certainly chilling if there is a chance it could be. One possible 'witness' has written to killing killers website, "I didn't make much of it at the time and didn't still until I moved to Minnesota and met a friend of one of the victims. When I was in college, in October 2000 I was found blacked out and vomiting. My memory is hazy but I'd met this guy who wanted me to follow him to another party. We walked on for several blocks and I kept asking where we were going. At first I was expecting the TKE house (Tau Kappa Epsilon Fraternity) but he said no. I asked if he was on the football team and he said no. He wouldn't tell me our destination. After a few more blocks I said I'd had enough and went home. In retrospect, where we were walking was toward the river that cut across campus, before I'd left him and gone... Made me scratch my head a little.'

Again, is his story true, or accurate? Although why would he make it up? There are other similar posts about men who say they have been separated by a group of both young men and women who they have met in bars. One of them talks about thinking something had been slipped into his drink and then resisted being pushed inside a van while walking along the street afterward. Another describes a man following him and then a van driving up fast and blocking his exit. There are numerous potential stories like this if they are looked for hard enough. Are these people just jumping on the bandwagon? Are any of these accounts true? Possibly they are.

Another weird account reads as follows, from a while before the current killings started, implying they could have been occurring a lot longer than perhaps realised.
"I attended high school in 1960, 1961 and 1962 in New York City. I have a strange story. A school mate Michael who I had lunch with is what this story is about..
Some things I definitely remember but generally some facts are vague to me. I definitely remember standing in front of the academic building at lunch time and speaking to Michael.
He said he had a boat and wanted me to go for a boat ride with him. (He may have indicated he had some friend that would also be there). He and his friends..
I believe prior to this meeting he had asked me what religion I was and I said Jewish.
I believe he confirmed this (insistently) once or twice..
At some point I believe he asked me if I could swim, also was I good swimmer..I would have said yes a good swimmer.
Michael then asked me to meet them in a specific location by the water in Brooklyn or Queens (one or the other).He said you know where that is and how to get there, I said no.. Then he asked about one or two more locations. I said no; he said take this train and that train; I said no, I am from the Bronx and I would get lost. Well he asked me, do I know any desolate area in

Brooklyn or Queens? I said no. How about the Bronx? I said yes City Island, Orchard Beach.
He thought about it but said he wouldn't know how to get home from there.
Here is where the story gets strange. Michael says to me "never mind, there's no boat," ... "we were going to lure you there and kill you! You are going to get me in a lot of trouble with my family" he said! "I was supposed to bring you there and kill you and now I am in trouble with my family." I was still trying to have lunch with him as he walked away mad at me because he was now going to get in trouble for not bringing the (prey) to the water edge!!!! and don't I understand.
At the time other than losing a friend (lunch buddy) this immediately rolled of my back like water on a ducks back and I did not think about it (or talk about it) for over 50 years...until now."
His story doesn't make a lot of sense in terms of the victims now and why such a group, if it existed, would be hunting and killing them as prey; but then it doesn't have to make sense to us; just them.

'TheyDontSee' posted on a facebook interest group,
'It's a group, both men and women, and government involved. It's co-ordinated. Victims aren't snatched; they're tricked then forcibly pulled into a van and subdued. It's serious (spiritual/occult) yet it's a game too. They use the internet to communicate but not 'publicly' on it. They're kept alive and groomed; brainwashing, mental torture, (not physically). They

have existed for decades. On the east it's killing with a gun, then they decided it was 'safer' to do it this way and they're right; we're still looking for them..'

Is this from an insider into some of the investigations? Or just a guess? Of course, there's every chance that some of the messages and opinions posted on the internet are from those within the groups itself. They are probably monitoring and reading it all.

A recent graduate of engineering, writes, 'I live in Wisconsin. The night I'm about to describe has nagged at me for almost two years now..I tried to ignore it but as one who always trusts my gut..While still in school I was at a bar one night not far from the house I was living in at the time. I used to like to go the bar and do my homework. I know this sounds odd but I can tune out my surroundings. I always sat at one end of the bar and worked on advanced math. This night I could feel someone's eyes, and looking up I saw a man sitting across from me. He was dressed very nice. We made eye contact and shivers went down my spine, but I went back to my work. A few minutes later I felt alarmed, as unbeknown to me the man had came and was sat right next to me. (There were other empty seats along the bar.) He attempted small talk. I told him I was in engineering school. This really got his interest, and he kept asking more and more questions. He seemed very impressed that I held a 3.5 GPA again it really aroused his interest. I presumed he must be gay and trying to hit on me. I answered his questions bluntly, trying to end the conversation. It did not end. He kept trying to make talk and buy me drinks. After I kept refusing my guard really started to go up. He'd told me he wasn't from round here but travelled through for business; then his story changed to having friends close-by and did I want to go to there and smoke pot with him. I did smoke pot; but I hadn't told him that and he looked real square. All my radars were going off.'

'Eventually, I went to the bathroom and slipped out the back door. A few months later I stumbled upon the murder theories and chills went down my spine. After much consideration I contacted the investigators and told them. I said I could give a good description for a police sketch, but nothing happened and they never contacted me again. The guy was creepy on so many different levels...and on a side note, the bar is just down from a secluded park by the river....'

Another lead, or just another strange story? Who was the smartly dressed man; and were there more like him waiting outside somewhere in the darkness?

What did one woman and her boyfriend see going on in the woods? Was it a result of their over-imagination, or was there some kind of hunting for humans going on? Was a cop or a 'pretend' cop possibly involved?

'I'm shaken right now and need to share what just happened.' That was the first sentence of an email sent to Piehl when she was investigating the ongoing cases. The woman and her boyfriend were walking their dog on the wooded paths around Lake Minnetonka in Minnesota. It was a hot summer evening, and the woods and Lake were busy with people jogging, walking, in boats on the lake and groups partying and drinking. It was late and getting dark as they were walking through the area, when suddenly "a big dark blue van pulled up on the roadside and stopped. Inside the man had the lights and he seemed to be typing or searching on a police -like scanner. My boyfriend and I got scared and so we began to run up the path. Just then a young man who looked to be in his twenties came walking past us. He was on his own and he looked afraid. We carried on down the path until the boy came running from behind us. When he reached us he stopped. I asked if he was okay and he replied that he wasn't and was frightened. He apologized for being so messed up and couldn't even begin to talk about it but that it was terrible.'

Then he walked off, away from the water and toward the road. The couple were concerned for him and they looked around to find where he had gone but they couldn't see. When they reached their parked car, they were about to drive off when they noticed a police cruiser. They flashed their headlights at the cop to draw his attention to get him to come over, but to their surprise the cop sped off and drove off toward the quieter part of the area. The couple dialled 911 from their car and gave information about their concerns. The woman says that the police didn't do anything, and now, "I am scared. I'm sure the boy was running away from the van. It is like the van was waiting for him; that it knew he would be walking that path and was waiting for him there. Was whoever it was in that van in contact with the cop and with other people in the area? I know it sounds crazy but I'm afraid now for the safety of that boy. I wish had told him to come with us; he looked terrified, but he could have been dangerous."

A young man writes in to a forum, wondering if he survived something which many more have not; 'I feel weird posting this, but I've never experienced something like this before; it may or may not be related. I don't have the proof. It may just be a case of someone putting something in my drink, and nothing else; but the number of people connected has me thinking there was a lot more to it than that. I'd left 2 friends inside the bar to go sit out on the deck. The weirdness started when two young females sat next to me and started telling me very flattering statements. This wouldn't normally be very strange, but there was a very weird vibe to it; they asked me more than once if I was there with anyone else. Male friends of theirs would occasionally come over while they were complimenting me, then they would disappear back inside the Bar. Then one of the females left with suddenly with no notice. It was at this point that the other female started acting strange toward me. She said at one point for me to quit yelling at her, as though I was screaming. She then tried to get me to go back to her place, which struck me as odd - it didn't seem like she was trying to pick me up. She wanted me to go to a party at her house. She got up to leave, and I told one of her male friends she was leaving if he wanted to catch her up. He said it didn't matter.'

'We (my friends and I) left the bar to go to another bar. I had a pretty good buzz going. That same male followed me to the next bar. He ordered a beer and gave it to me. It tasted weird. We followed a girl that he saw and said he liked, outside. After having a shot, it gave me a really uneasy feeling, but I thought I was just buzzed. I went inside and ordered more shots and beer. Then the Bar was closing and we were kicked out. Something happened to me outside of the bar; that may or may not be considered a crime...but..I'll leave that.'

'We, for some reason, followed some guys down the street to their house. They went inside and locked their door so my friend and I started heading away, along with the other guy. My friend was now about five hundred feet away when we got back to the Bar. He later said that he felt it was as though they were trying to separate us. The guy from the first bar suddenly grabs me, and proceeds to try and push me in his vehicle. I'm not a small guy, so this was not going to be an easy thing for him to do. As I was telling him that he was soon going to have a problem, he noticed my friend walking up the street closer now. I'm pretty sure if my friend had been there, he would have used a different method to get me in that vehicle. I ran weaving in an out of yards, and then I had noticed that the same guy was now driving around back and forth trying to find me. I have never had a team of people try to do this.'

This next case is taken from local Newspaper reports, including New Jersey.com, in an area where, as described at the beginning of the book, just in the last few months, Zachary Marr disappeared, and Matthew Genovese, Anthony Urena, Dennis Njoroge, and Eric Munsell have all been found dead in the water. According to a later Hoboken police report, just before 2 a.m. in March 2014, three men who were walking in a park heard yelling. At first, the men said they didn't think too much of it; until the yelling turned to screams for help. They called the police who arrived to find a man in the nearby Hudson River, clinging desperately to a concrete pylon in the ice-cold water by Pier C (near to where Matthew Genoese was found dead in the water). Managing to rescue him by tossing a rope out to him, the police pulled him out of the water and took him to the Hospital, where he was treated for hypothermia. His name was Ryan Lee, 24, and he told the police that three men who he did not know, had thrown him into the river.

He told the police officers that he had been in a club called Boa, and that after he left, he was attacked by three men *all dressed in black,* who threw him into the Hudson River. It was on the night of St Patrick's Day celebrations; again, on a holiday or day of celebration, as is the common recurring theme.

Of course, the three men in black could have easily been just regular guys having a drink and, after drinking too much, decided in an inebriated state, on a night of celebrations, that it would be fun to throw someone in the river. The men have never been identified. Lee told the officers that he had left the Club after getting into a fight with his girlfriend, and that he had left his girlfriend and the friends he was with inside the club. What's curious is the way that Lee describes his attackers, as "Three men dressed in black." Was this just their fashion? Or weather related attire? Or, is the implication here that it was more like they were actually dressed for an operation of a black nature; literally, a black ops?

Could this also be the case for another young man, called Sunil Tripathi; except that not only did Sunil end up dead in the river, but there is perhaps the chance that quite possibly he was actually used in a 'black ops' prior to his death? Taking into account what an ex-private detective recently told me; Tomich Carpenter, who started a spreadsheet, gathering data to analyze for possible patterns in these cases; he believes he's found several similarities between the drowned men;

"I believe these students attended 'public' seminars and anyone interested were asked to stay after the meeting to learn more. That's where the recruitment started. Later, people turned up drowned to scare those already indoctrinated to remain in."

It's a very good theory, and those who now wanted no part of it, once they discovered what it was really about, once they had got in too deep, but now knew too much about the existence of this 'group,' they were the ones who were killed-off.

"These young men would fit into any community they were assigned to, to await further instruction. Money could be enticement (as could status and recognition of their abilities as scholars and sportsmen initially) the hook that attracted them, and death could be punishment. Those that did not turn up drowned are living in other communities with new identities. This is a national security issue and I believe black ops is involved."

When I put this possibility to a criminal profiler, his answer was that while he had no proof anything like that was going on, he did not doubt it's validity as a possible explanation. As for Sunil, his family went through not only having to suffer his death, but when he went missing, he was also falsely accused of something heinous. But it doesn't end there. In fact, as many controversial researchers have explicitly said, it appears that in their opinion, he was quite possibly used in a false flag attack. It began in a very strange twist of events, when Sunil, in his absence, was named as a suspect in the Boston bombing of April 15, 2013. After the bombing, late in the night, a policeman on the police scanner named him as he was one of the suspects being sought. Within seconds, his name was appearing all over the internet, on Reddit, and other social media sites, followed rapidly by news agencies.

The problem was, as would later be discovered, there didn't seem to be a recording existing of the police scanner conversation mentioning Sunil. The recording exists; it's just that his name is not heard being said at all. Mystery and conspiracy deepened after this, because no-one could really understand how this young man came to be enemy number one in the first place. The official story seemed to be that a girl from his high school identified him from pictures taken at the scene of the bombing, and it grew from there. His parents were astonished and horrified that their quiet student son attending Brown University was being hunted as one of the Boston bombers.

Later, it would be suggested from some non-msn sources, that his name was deliberately arranged to be used. Why would this be? Well, he looks remarkably like one of the Chechen brothers accused of the bombings. This alleged 'false flag' event has been deconstructed by some serious alternative researchers, who clearly dispute the official version of events that took place. They believe, mainly from the many photographs and videos taken on the day; that the two bombers were, in their opinion, not the real bombers at all. They also feel it entirely possible that the boys were switched at various times; and this would be where Sunil comes in. He bore a remarkable resemblance to one of the two Chechen brothers later held responsible. Sunil looked like the young brother, Dzhokhar Tsarnaev.

Sunil's name went viral; but as thousands of heavily armed law enforcement officers moved in on a twenty block area of Watertown in Boston, searching for him, they brought out their suspect following a shoot-out and it only resulted in more confusion. The young man they arrested was not Sunil; it was the Chechen, Dzhokhar, who was later sentenced to prison for the terrorist attack. The area of Watertown had been under complete lock-down; an unprecedented move for modern American citizens, where a terrorist attack had resulted in a strictly imposed curfew, with residents in that area being told not to leave their homes, and the rest of the town told to get home and stay home. The Chechen had survived an earlier shootout in the area with police, during which his brother, Tamerlan, had been killed. Ironically, it wasn't until after the lockdown had been lifted that a Watertown resident came across the suspect hiding in the man's boat in his backyard.

Of course, the police said they were conducting a manhunt for Sunil Tripathi. Or was it for Dzhokhar? And, why, when later photographs were scrutinized by alternative media sources, did they point out that in some of the photographs taken on the day, someone looking very much like Sunil appeared to be in some of the scenes.

The implied, and in some sources, the explicit accusation, came out that Sunil had been used as some kind of 'double' or indeed even 'patsy' at the scene of the bombings. The subject of the bombings, which some have called 'false flags' is one that is hotly controversial, and indeed, some outspoken critics of the official version are now no longer alive. A coincidence? That's entirely possible, but some in the alternative investigative field would reply that that in itself only strengthens the claims that all was not as it seemed at the bombing.

The fact is, at the time of the Boston Bombing, Sunil had already been declared a missing person. He had vanished from his Brown University apartment. He'd last been seen in the early morning of March 16, 2013, just after 1.30 a.m. close by to his apartment building, which was not far from the University campus. He was a 22 year old student there, although he had recently taken time out from his Philosophy course to cope with what his family described as minor depression. His grades at the time were very high. He was known as a deep critical thinker, and an excellent chess player. Though he was said to be suffering from depression, he had not been formally diagnosed as having it, and he was taking no medication for it.

He appeared to have left his apartment without his phone, wallet, or his mode of transport; the bicycle he used to get around town and college. He was later said to have left behind a short note; a quote from a well-known classic book, which the authorities took to believe was a suicide note. Prior to his disappearance, his family said that he had gone out with his roommates and drunk only tea. On his return to his apartment, he had talked with his grandmother on the phone, and then chatted by text with his aunt until late. Both of them said that nothing seemed to be troubling him, and nothing he said caused had given them any reason for concern.

Just after 1.30 a.m. a surveillance camera appears to capture a man resembling his appearance, walking along the sidewalk, away from the apartment. Just prior to leaving the apartment he had been on his computer.

That was the last sighting of him. His body was discovered 38 days later, on April 23th, floating in the river off India Point Park, in the town of Providence. He had to be identified by dental records.

How he ended up in the river is a mystery. So too is the allegation made by some in the alternative media that he was somehow involved in the Boston Bombing. It must be explained here that when they say he was somehow involved; they do not mean willingly, or with real knowledge. Their implication is very clear. They are saying that he was somehow used. He was role playing perhaps, like a 'crisis actor' who some allege are often used at the site of 'false flags.' If he was playing a role however, he had no idea it would end in his death. They are not saying he was responsible in any way for the actual bombing; rather that he was acting on the stage for them, playing his part in the complex and purposely manipulated 'truth' of how the authorities wanted the event to be seen.

There is the possibility here then that Sunil could have either willingly participated in the game, believing perhaps that this was some kind of drill or practice for such a scenario; or he could even have been forced into playing a role. He may have been 'recruited' by an 'organization' to play the part of a double for the real bomber (who again, some sources believe was not the real bomber either, but a patsy). He could have believed he was playing a benevolent role, assisting the security services in their fight against terrorist threats; or he could have been 'recruited' under this guise, without knowing that those who recruited him, had no compunction in using him in such a way that he would have to be disposed of afterward, because by then he would know too much.

His death was ruled as 'suicide' despite suicide by drowning not being a very common method for men to chose at all, and despite it being a very difficult way to kill oneself. Additionally, again, bodies tend to float to the surface after about 10 days. It was his University rowing coach who spotted his body floating in the river; which implies that it was obviously a regularly used and busy part of the river; yet it took a long time for his body to be found. The implication here is then very clear. Either he had been walking the streets homeless and penniless for quite a number of days prior to his death, 38 in fact, or he'd been 'somewhere' before he ended up dead in the water. He had no wallet and had not been in contact with his family.

He disappeared 3 weeks prior to the bombings, and he was found 8 days after it. Where had he been? He had to be identified by his dental records, which implies he had been in the water for some time, and yet if he had, why had his body not surfaced sooner? Or, he had been killed elsewhere and then placed in the water? With the 'official version' being that he was so badly decomposed he could not be identified any other way than by his dental records, this would mean that his actual body itself then was not i.d. then?

On the other hand, is this just all the product of a conspiracy minded way of thinking? Is this once more an example of how easy it can be to lose objectivity in the search for the answer? Again, it's entirely possible.

Interestingly though, Geopolitical analyst Tony Cartalucci, on his *LandDestroyer* blog, says of the involvement of the F.B.I. in searching for the missing man; "It's not uncommon for the FBI to aid in searches for missing people; however, that this 'false lead' of the alleged identity of the bombing suspects, (that of both Sunil and the Chechen boys) involved cases the FBI was working on already, before the bombings, raises immense suspicion. The Chechen brothers were reportedly already known to the authorities, and, prior to the bombing, the F.B.I. were also searching for Sunil."

This of course is all speculation and is likely to be entirely wrong; but what it does do is raise the spectre of the possibility that some of the missing or later found drowned young men are being used in some fashion after having been recruited.

An eyewitness, Greg Van Haessler, in Watertown on the night of the search for the escaped 'suspect,' Sunil, says, "They had him in custody behind my house; he looked exactly like Sunil Tripathi. This was during the city-wide 'lock-down' when everyone was told to stay indoors after the bombing, while the police went in search of the bombers. Others have gone through the photos of the Marathon prior to the bombing and there is a widespread belief that someone looking very much like Sunil is visible standing in the VIP area on the route of the Marathon." Van Haesler posted that night on facebook, stating that he believed this was a staged event. He says that after he did that, a SWAT team entered his house and took him away for a short period of time. Is he telling the truth too? In this age of misinformation and disinformation, it is really impossible to say.

Was the young man depressed and drowned himself, in an act that is not easy, unless he weighed himself down; a detail that, if he did, does not appear in the autopsy result or the police statements, or was he victim to an unidentified group who may be behind the many deaths like his?

Does Sunil's case offer the possibility of shedding light on what could perhaps be one motive of this supposed group? While some of the evidence appears to lean toward a metaphysical, theosophical or 'religious motive;' the idea that a unit exists for the purpose of using some of these boys who are missing until discovered dead, for a political motive, is highly disturbing, if there is any possibility it could of course really be true. What of the case of James Holmes and the Aurora Batman massacre? According to many non-MSM media sources, "The first report of suspects was that of *two men* fleeing the movie theatre, both wearing backpacks"
Who were those two men? Were these reports wrong?

'James Holmes was mind controlled,' came the allegations. 'James Holmes was kidnapped,'
And what of the other reports of "three people dragging an unknown person into a plain vehicle and leaving at speed."

The reports were of course referring to the Batman Movie Theatre shooting, in Aurora, Colorado.
"Two months before this massacre, James Holmes world was turned upside down," says Grace Powers, an independent researcher who some say is onto something, and others ridicule or say she is 'misinformation.' Nevertheless, her particular version of the Batman Aurora shooting is a wild but interesting tale.

"Two months before this massacre, James Holmes world was turned upside down. That's when two 'black ops' hitmen entered his life and unravelled it using a drug called Scopolamine."

Scopolamine, otherwise known as 'Devil's Breath' is an insanely powerful drug. It's odourless, tasteless and in fact was recently in the headlines when the U.K. Daily Mail reported on its use in a series of robberies on tourists by a criminal gang who were simply blowing it into the face of unsuspecting passers by, and rendering them instantaneously and completely under their power. The drug acts in such a way as to make the victim wholly unable to resist doing anything the perpetrators ask of them.

In this case, it was being used to get the tourists to hand over their credit cards, and even getting them to the nearest bank, to withdraw all of their money and hand it over 'willingly, without any resistance, to the members of the criminal gang. They would also be walked back to their hotel rooms, where they would hand over all of their valuable possessions on request. After the fact, they would have absolutely no recollection whatsoever of what they had done.

Toxicology expert Miriam Gutierrez says "From a medical point of view, it's the perfect drug because the victim won't remember anything."

In effect, the drug turns a person into a willing and totally compliant zombie who will do anything requested of them. We have a twofold possibility here then; firstly, it would be the perfect drug to be used on these young men who are being found in the water. Secondly, it could also be used on them to make them do something terrible; to make them drown someone else. The drug renders complete inability to resist orders or commands. It enables someone to kill themselves, compliantly, willingly, and without any resistance, fight or struggle. Alternately, it could also be used to turn someone into an 'assassin,' to carry out the drowning deaths. It is food for thought indeed.

Expert on this drug, Dr. Camilo Uribe says, "it destroys the power of reasoning; there is no power to think or to reason."

In fact, the drug is nothing new; it was used by the C.I.A. and both German and American scientists as a truth serum, and to enable the scientists to conduct any number of inhumane experiments. With Nazi scientists allegedly brought over in Operation Paperclip, some U.S. scientists too were forced into coercion and made to drug unknowing victims, ranging from prisoners, politicians, and crime bosses; the latter two being drugged in order to blackmail them after the fact, once caught in compromising positions. Sometimes even the scientists were drugged too, resulting in at least one jumping out of a hotel window to his death.

What's worrying, is that it could be used both by the perpetrators, to make the young men self-destruct by drowning themselves; and it could be used on other young men to turn them into killers who would willingly but unknowingly drown another young man, and they would never even know that what they had done. Of course, again we enter the realms of wild speculation and conjecture, but still.

According to the Daily Mail, "It's ordoless, tasteless and can put on food, or dissolved into drinks. Women have been drugged and gang-raped or rented out. A common scenario is that it's put in a person's drink and they wake up miles away, with no memory of what has happened. The drug temporarily blocks the brain's ability to form memories; which also makes it impossible to later identify those who have given them the drug."

So, crucially here, even if it was being given to these young men by 'someone,' they would never be able to identify who had given it to them.

Says controversial researcher Grace Powers, "This is what happened to James Holmes.' (Although others will say that he had a history of psychiatric problems and was taking medication) 'He claims he has no memory of the massacre or what happened. He was reportedly arrested at his car without any resistance. The rear of his car window was broken. Why? Had he been locked inside the car? Why did the police have to smash the window to access him?"

She continues, "Eight weeks before the shooting, Hitman 1 moves in with him after drugging him. He keeps him in a permanently drugged state, and accesses his internet and emails as well as bank. He buys the guns using Holmes's I.D. He booby traps the apartment. He dyes Holmes's hair red. He creates a profile on a dating site stating Holmes's is 6 feet tall; he doesn't know he's in fact 6 feet 3 inches. He uses the notebook to sketch details of the shooting plan. He mails it to a Professor."

"He drives the getaway car to the Movies and parks it. He enters the Movie Theatre for the Dark Night. His phone rings; its Hitman number 2. Number 1 goes to the emergency door and opens it,' as Grace Powers says, 'this according to witness Corbin Dates, who was inside the Movie Theatre."

Then the massacre begins, according to her, with Holmes still locked in the car. "Was Holmes involved in a real-life Jason Bourne 'Project Treadstone'?" Powers asks, referring to the fictional films and books by Robert Ludlum.

She also adds that he was a research assistant at Salk Institute, at the University of California in La Jolla, who happened to be working with both DARPA, and Wisconsin University, as well as other Universities and a confectionary company, on a project using the antioxidant flavanol to test the improvement of combat troop fatigue through its use. The project she says was led by DARPA as part of a performance program which 'involved engineering brain-machine interfaces for battlefield.'

Nothing sinister there surely? It's just a natural ingredient; flavanol, found in foods. What this does do however, is introduce the idea that Universities do and may well be working on research projects in association with military or government and private corporations, and this is often probably not widely known. And, as will later be discussed, when MK Ultra was exposed, 149 sub-projects were found to be have been operating at University campuses across the USA.

As the retired private detective Tomich said, he believes these boys attend some kind of recruiting seminars on campus, and that unknowingly, they join an 'organization' and are killed as an example to others who may wish to leave once they realize what they have joined; that these young men are 'recruited' into an organization, without any real awareness of what this organization really stands for; and that once they are in, they cannot leave, for doing so would mean certain death or imprisonment, after they are implicated in 'involvement' in these drowning, even if just by association.

They are then 'in' for life; and become very useful tools for that organization to use for any purpose, no matter how dark or evil. They are forced to stay in it while others are drowned and they are then blackmailed into staying in; once they have witnessed and thereby been implicated as an accessory to a murder, it is used as a terrifying threat that it will happen to them if they try to leave, and if they go to the authorities about it, they will be held accountable for murder.

"These young men would await further instruction. Money could be enticement and death could be punishment. Those that did not turn up drowned are living in other communities with new identities. This is a national security issue and I believe a black ops government group is involved."

An alternate theory to this is that the abductions and murders are pre-emptive strikes, to take out the future leaders, the most up-coming and promising of students who could go on to join political bodies and have an influence that this group do not want encouraged.

Interestingly, one man recently contacted me after listening to a radio show I appeared on talking about these drowning deaths. He contacted me to tell me about his own inexplicable disappearance, and at the same time, he also told me something very strange about the Aurora Batman shootings. Matt's background is that he has been a successful creator of RPG's (Role Playing Computer Games) Comic Books, and movies. He learnt film production at the AFI, (American Film Institute) in Los Angeles. While there, he says,

"In 2008, at the AFI 'The Dark Knight' was screened while it was still in movie theatres, with a Q&A session from the production designer. The designer was Nathan Crowley; heir of Aleister. (Aleister Crowley was Nathan's Grandfather's cousin.) He warned me about the "Dark Knight Rises shooting" *4 years in advance*. And the map of Bane that shows "Sandy Hook;" the propmaster (who I met) dies in a mysterious car crash in...Newton Connecticut?!"

With regards to the 'Smiley faces," whether accepted as evidence or not, he says that it struck a chord with him, for a very specific reason. "The classic Smiley face has connotations to MK Ultra. I used to channel the

Smiley Face at age 13, (1987) as a child of Montauk myself, and having had some experience of mind-control (Hollywood Montauk) it feels 'true' to me. I can't say anything concrete, but I offer those dots connected."

"As for my 411-ish vanishing from the schoolyard (with many witnesses) I have found that Montauk did it with technology. But I would say that from experience, all of the water-bodies, the 411-stuff, sounds like interdimensional abduction right out of the old fairytales. Fairy rings, etc."

"Of my disappearance, I returned a few hours later, borderline hypothermia, despite having a jacket and it being a warm May day. In the 1990's, amidst the alien abduction peer-pressure, I held out, telling everyone it was a different experience, more "interdimensional" (though I certainly believe aliens and abductions occur, but just that my experience was more "passing between the veils between worlds") not to another dimension. It sounds weird, and I resisted it for decades, until confirming with others in the field. I never claimed to be abducted. Just "the curtain went down between dimensions, and we saw one another". But looking into those eyes.....I saw...."everything."

He continues, "Sorry if this is a bit disconnected; I've been around and my thoughts are a little rattled these days. I have a history of "my art being imitated by later-life". I've made comic books, RPG games, movies, all kinds of expression over 30 years. In the 1980s I just used that Smiley Face a lot, before it was popular. It "felt right" when I was in "that mood", which I would now call on the edge of an "altar"(ego)."

"But I have a tendency to 'get things right;" way beyond synchronicity. My games and novels and film scripts- all registered years ago - accurately contain things from Masonic rituals to current events. It's....weird. So, I go with my gut a lot, and my gut says look into some sort of government mind-control for whoever is behind the bar-drink-abduction scenario. The Montauk Boys had a similar treatment in the 1970s. They were abducted to the base, and disposed of; Long Island New York. Naziland. Teslaland. Brookhaven. Stargates. All wrapped up in a nice little CIA swastika paperclip-bow...Sorry, I get a bit emotional."

"The Montauk Project was taking Tesla-tech, from the Phil-Exp and, with a UFO chair (or some sort of chair), amplifying the psychic powers of specific frequency "Aryan" children -- Mostly Nordic, with some Native American blood, for the right DNA vibration. They found they could open stargates. For the longest time, they abducted kids from Long Island. But eventually, they started doing 'remote grabs'."

"In 1983 (and I have a lot of backup data, not just claims) I was one of those "remote grabbed". At least, that is my present theory, but all the evidence points to it. And resisting the "attention" and enduring the REAL ridicule of saying "no, this was not an alien abduction" for twenty years, I'm not one to jump to conclusions. I can prove (documented) I did vanish from my schoolyard with over 100 witnesses in 1983, at the same time they were doing the remote grabs, and my pedigree is like Montauk Boy 1,000%, from blood to my very synchronously unique Hollywood background – the AFI (American Film Institute), and my mentors were in the OTO, Masons, and "stargate" programs and films (from Ghostbusters to Back to the Future, which actually all have the same occult connections) Yes, I had my *Eyes Wide Shut* offers down there, met the big people, and have further confirmation."

"Following the Crowley/Parsons/Hubbard/JPL (Jet Propulsion Laboratory) /MK-Ultra path, from Hollywood to Brookhaven. It's quite a tight little satanic circle. And I'm not Christian. I'm more George Carlin or John Cleese when it comes to religion. But the Hollywood/military complex very much are luciferian at the top. My fiancé worked inside Disneyland, Club "33" and all that. It's all true, sad to say."

"There is a very real military-occult-CIA-mind control element connecting Hollywood, Montauk, and vanishing people. I really do believe at some level we (abuse that technology, and have for some time, perhaps in some alliance with "them"; I can't say. But the Hollywood elite believe this. I've been there. (I have some Lucas film inside stories, all the way to the Grove.)"

"I see no reason why this same agenda or something similar could not be behind the 'missing 411' in general. Maybe the aliens/fairies do it, and so do we now, to some degree."

"In Los Angeles, 2011, when my relationship/career was ending, my then-fiancé liked to hike the Griffith and nearby trails. I did not, having a fear of snakes. But, one day, we went (her choice) to the Arroyo watershed, just north of the Rose Bowl. There, having at the time no knowledge of anything related to Parson/Hubbard/Crowley/JPL/ OTO, somehow I felt a wave of "bad energy" go into me."

"I felt sick. Nauseous, and grouchy. For a month after, I kept threatening to jump off our roof (it had a 5-story sundeck) and die. I only learned later about "Suicide Bridge" just South of Arroyo/Rose Bowl, where since 1913, over 200 people have jumped to their deaths, all compelled by the forces of what the natives called 'Devil's Gate.' Where Crowley and co. did their OTO ritual to summon "Lam", the Gray alien-like demon."

"Stargates." "Oz", they call it. Octagon. Namesake of the Swiss bankers and portal-occultism. Crowley, also, tied to that Laurel Canyon crowd, AND the Montauk project, And Hubbard? His apprentice? He started the Scouts and park's trails in the 1920s here in Tacoma..."

"I've lost . . . all the usual (fiancé, career, etc) for sticking to my story. I don't say these things lightly. I know they sound fantastic, but someday I hope to put all my papers in order and make my case. To some extent I am afraid. I have had "reprisals". "Bad luck" when I talk too much. I really think though, largely, people are taken to other worlds. Many of the water-deaths, just like in medieval days, and before. "They" have always been with us. But for my part, the Montauk thing, that in itself is a human mechanical contrivance; but the experience feels so similar -- the dimensional displacement. I used to not believe so much in fairytales . . . I've had to reconsider."

"In a Tesla-based cosmos, an electromagnetic matrix of consciousness, it seems frequency is indeed everything, including slipping between worlds. When people are on their phone -- then silence? Maybe they just do indeed vanish. I did."

When I asked Matt if he thought the disappearances had anything to do with Genes; "Genetics? Probably in the usual "elite" search for purity-of-blood. My film school thesis having been *Indiana Jones*, oddly. . . I changed the Grail Chapel to Rosslyn Chapel, and that DNA spiral column which "contains the Holy Grail". I think the whole Templar-Mason-Scottish Rite lives on, and they definitely do in Hollywood, seeking that "Skywalker" type blood."

"Perhaps military funding goes towards depopulation, ultimately, and Eugenics. Deep down, I think the traditions of the OTO and Mystery Schools are alive and well, seeking transhumanism. They use the military and science to their own ends, even as higher, nonhuman powers use them. Like Sauron using Saruman in Lord of the Rings. I equate non-human powers with Mordor, and the Illuminati-types as Isengard. They "think" they can win, ignoring all classic wisdom, so they fund mad-scientists everywhere."

"Harmonics . . . True magic. Frequency. Psychology. Powerful weapon on the unsuspecting. I often wonder if the whole matrix isn't some game we're all playing? So many names, numbers and things line up these days, it's like we're being toyed with."

"I really think the veils are thinning more and more. And with things like Hollywood having mass manifestation rituals, along with hard control like Haarp/chemtrails, and big guns like CERN, we are witnessing merging dimensions. Certainly the whole Vril/Nazi/OTO/Hollywood gang (extended to the UN, CFR, etc) is on 'The Dark Side.'"

"But ultimately, I think what rules the "Illuminati" is the Cult of Saturn. Certainly those Masons in the Big Club consider degree 33 to be the level you pledge to Lucifer. But they believe by that point that Lucifer is a good guy. Bill Cooper's Mystery Babylon series, in my opinion, is spot-on to their thinking. The Hollywood/DC

Illuminati are twisted enough to seek the Light/Lux, etc. As Connery said at the end of Indiana Jones and the Last Crusade: He found..."Illumination." It IS like "Eyes Wide Shut." It's secret. And secrecy breeds corruption. They cover it up like they cover up everything else in their glamorous, very phony world -- they become cult-addicts, justifying their fix with "you're not initiated, it's okay to lie to you"."

"Watching the police state rise around us on both sides of the Pond . . . It seems like Star Wars made real, with an Empire, a rising Rebellion, and even some magic thrown in there. What do they cover-up? What truly paranormal forces are we dealing with that they only presume to control? MK was/is definitely at work in Hollywood. Manchurian Candidates everywhere "above the line" -- I've looked into a lot of soulless eyes down there."

Matt's account, to those who have never experienced any of the things he has, may sound wild, but his perception of the way some things are, is fully validated by many scholars in this field.

Chapter 10:
Something Getting Into Their Heads

Recalling now the case of engineering graduate Ewan Curbeam, mentioned briefly earlier in the book, he was Airman of the year and poster boy for a National Guard recruiting campaign, who had gone out with some friends to a Bar in Baltimore City on a Friday night in November 2013. He decided to leave the Bar before his friends, and said he was heading home. He was seen heading toward where he had parked his car; surely an indication that in his case, he certainly wasn't drunk or he wouldn't have been getting back in his car to drive. He never made it to his car; it was found still parked in the same spot he'd left it in. It was less than half a mile from the Bar he'd been in. It wasn't parked beside the river. A few days later he was found dead in the river.

It's interesting that he along with quite a few of the other young men were studying advanced engineering. Again, maybe nothing, but another person who was an advanced engineering specialist comes to mind, for a specific reason that perhaps one has to also look more deeply into no, as will be explained shortly.

When writing 'Taken in the Woods' I covered the tragic case of the mass suicides of young people that had been happening in the Bridgend area of Wales, a small town surrounded by woods and moorland and approximately an hour's drive from the Brecon Beacons National Park. By the start of 2012, 79 young people had hung themselves in rapid succession, always using the same method, by hanging themselves. It's likely that these deaths are still happening, as some alternative journalists believe, but it's not being reported because of a D-notice, to keep a sense of calm, or as a cover-up some suggest. A couple of the young people were unsuccessful in hanging themselves, although they tried. When asked why they had done it, they said that a voice in their head had told them it was what they should do, and that if they did it, everything would be alright. Neither had any prior signs of mental illness.

So, the question I posed was, had something got into their heads somehow? The theories and possible evidence are discussed in that book, however, one particularly relevant possibility was explained, despite it being one that would appear rather outlandish, and of course, remains entirely unproven, or does it?

When the mainstream media covered what was happening, some alternative researchers speculated that something had to be getting into the heads of these young people for it to be such an unprecedented cluster. The speculation was that it wasn't their own voices telling them to kill themselves, it was some form of weaponized electronics. Voice to skull, or ELF waves for example. Voice to Skull isn't a new thing. So, the question is, could some form of sound or vibrational energy weapons also be being used on some of these men? As some form of testing? To get them to do things, willingly?

Although sometimes there is clear evidence of very high levels of alcohol or drugs such as GHB in their systems, what about the ones who don't have anything in their system? Or the ones who are running scared but don't know what they are running from? Or the ones who have no memory of how they ended up in the water, as will be described later.

Where is the evidence of such 'weapons' even existing though? In 'Taken in the Woods,' I quoted physicist Barrie Trower, who alleges he was a former MI5 Agent and who makes the claim that he has first hand knowledge of the sinister use of scalar waves; microwaves in Wi-Fi and telecom Masts. He claims that intelligence agencies have misused microwaves to negatively influence people, from triggering heart attacks to taking control of a person's mind by reading their thoughts, and then changing their thoughts. They can remotely control someone without the person ever knowing it, and people can be programmed to kill, or kill themselves, he claims.
"It is easy to make people hear voices in their skulls. This is not mental illness," he says, "its technology."

His outrageous claim is that 'thousands of innocent people,' have been used as guinea pigs, and he believes the testing of psychotronic weapons has been extensively carried out.

Then there's Tim Rifat PhD, whose work is in the study of mind control technology, and who quotes Dr Ross Adey of 'Project Pandora,' whose behaviour modification experiments, he says, used ELF on the exact frequency as the current systems such as TETRA use, and that Adey's experiments 'caused frenzied emotional imbalance.'

As cited by several books on the topic, the USAF Scientific Board published their own report back in 1996 stating that, from their study of how the brain can be manipulated,'It's possible to create speech in the human body, for the possibility of covert suggestion.'

Dr John Hall is renowned as a specialist in this field and has himself explained how subversive agencies can even directly access laptops and computers to remotely target the emotions of those using them.
"Nothing is too far-fetched now," he says. He cites Michael Persinger, expert in behavioural neuroscience, as having once said he could himself quite confidently control every brain on the planet. Dr Hall says that when someone suddenly starts hearing a voice in their head, telling them to do something to themselves, or to others, it can also be done by 'audio spotlight;' "A hand held device zoning in to focus only on you, so that no-

one else around you can hear it even though they are walking right beside you;" - in a street, in a wilderness area; anywhere..

Is there really some kind of human experimentation going on here? Using the technology on a specifically narrow target group to see if it were possible to cause self destruction en-masse but only in a certain type of demographic? Is this some kind of sick test run? But surely it would have been proven effective and stopped being used by now? Or is this all just an over-wrought imagination here?

Getting back to the engineering students, as well as engineering graduate Evan Curbeam's mysterious death in October 2013, *Whiteoutpress.com* reported "The Truth about the voices the Navy shooter in D.C. had complained about."
The 'Navy Shooter,' was a graduate in advanced engineering.
'When Intel employee Aaron Alexis opened fire at the Washington DC Naval Yard, killing 12, he'd spent weeks warning anyone who'd listen that the US Government was infiltrating his brain with voices.' It continues, "Unbelievable as this sounds, the military has had that exact weapon for decades."
Alexis was said to be an expert in electronics in the Navy and had been contracted to a private organization for what *Whitehousepress* call 'spy operations.'

Although he had a record for lateness on occasion, there were no other blemishes on his personnel file and he had certainly never been diagnosed with suffering form any form of mental illness. He took no medication for any psychiatric problems and his family said he had never shown any signs of psychological abnormality.

However, a month before he went on a killing rampage at the Nay Yard in D.C. he had repeatedly started telling friends and his co-workers that he was being targeted by a covet mind control weapon. He claimed to be a victim of a "brainwashing" program in which he could hear voices that no-one else could. When he told other people he could hear the voices and asked if they could hear them, they all said they could not.

He began to believe they were coming through the walls and the ceilings. He shot the ceiling in the hotel room he was living in, trying to stop the incessant voices. He went to the police, telling them that he couldn't sleep in his room because the voices being sent into his head were invading his mind and frightening him. He said it was being done by microwave. Being an expert in electronic systems, he also probably knew exactly how that was possible. After the shooting at the Yard, the FBI found the notes he'd written.

"Ultra-low frequency attack I have been subjected to for the last three months has driven me to this," he wrote. Then he went and bought a sawn off shot-gun.

Before using it to kill people at the Base, he scratched an engraving on the side of the gun. It said, "End to the torment."

The journal went on to investigate whether there really were weapons out there that could do this to a person. In a cached website by the military that they claim they found, a disturbing array of 'non-lethal' weapons are described, that had been developed for use by the military, including a "mind penetration device for 'voice-to-skull' communication," which consisted of the means to convert a human voice into a silent microwave pulse, with the words then able to be heard and understood subliminally in the targeted person's head.

The cached website explained that it had been developed for such purposes as 'to frighten birds from airport runways.' Perhaps we could also add then, that it could just as easily be used to 'frighten' humans; and by implication, could make them panic, run, in fear of their lives, terrorized by what was happening to them and trying to flee the area that they were hearing it in? Accidents then, could quite naturally follow, in their haste to flee. Death even, if they were in an area where the terrain was less easy to traverse; like a forest, wood, national park, or by a river. It could cause them and even suggest to them to carry out acts that are irrational. To flee, fall, die.

This form of weaponized abuse of course, doesn't just necessarily have to apply to victims; or rather, some of the victims could indeed be perpetrators too. Whoever the perpetrators are, it could be being used on them too. Journalist James Moore alleges that the CIA has long since mastered a technology called 'Rhic-edom,' or, 'Radio Hypnotic Intra-cerebral Control n Electronic Dissolution of Memory.'

The disturbing capabilities of this are alleged to be that it can remotely induce hypnotic trance, deliver suggestions to the subject, and even worse, it can erase all memory for both the period in which the instructions are given to the subject, and during the time that the subject is carrying out those instructions they have been asked to perform.

Operation Mind Control, by Walter H. Bowart, which was written nearly four decades ago, in 1978, claimed that Mind control "slaves" of the intelligence community; such as witnesses, couriers, and assassins could be "protected" from their own memories and any guilt by this amnesia. These "slaves" may be left alive, he says, but the knowledge they possess is buried deep within the tombs of their own minds by techniques which can keep the truth hidden even from those who have witnessed it.

People can be tasked with abducting, torturing, and killing other people, their targets, and have no recollection of having done it.

Dr. Robert Becker comments, "Such a device has obvious applications in covert operations designed to drive a target crazy with 'voices' or deliver undetectable instructions to a programmed assassin."

"I can hypnotize a man—without his knowledge or consent—into committing treason against the US Government," boasted Dr. George Estabrooks, in the early 1940s.

One expert, Professor Allan Scheflin, who wrote 'Mind Manipulators,' took the suggestion further in his research, and came to believe there was a link between so called 'satanic crimes' which were instead being carried out by retired black ops on behalf of the CIA.

So far, the question hasn't been asked, is there the possibility that alien entities are taking these young men; returning some of them and never returning others? There doesn't appear to be any clear evidence of this, or of harvesting of organs. However, interestingly, Martin Cannon claims that even those who believe they have been a victim of alien abduction may well instead have been the victim of some of this exotic technology just described.

When Cannon wrote 'The Controllers; A new hypothesis of Alien Abduction,' in 1990, he claimed to have read over 200,000 pages of documents from organizations including the CIA, and the Department of Defence, as wells as letters, statements and witness testimonies, and from this, he believed he had found that a person's mind could be controlled so that they believed they had gone through an encounter with alien entities.

"The kidnapping is real; the fear is real. The pain is real. But little grey men from Zeti Reticuli are not real; they are constructs; Halloween masks to disguise the real faces."

Crucially, what he also says is "Evidence exists linking members of the Intel community; CIA, Naval Intelligence, DARPA, with esoteric technology of mind control."

"For decades, 'spychiatrists' have been working behind the scenes - on college campuses. They have experimented with the erasing of memory, hypnotic resistance to torture, hypnotic suggestion, microwave induction of "voices," and a host of even more disturbing tech."

What's more, when MK Ultra was uncovered, there were 149 sub-projects operating on College Campuses. Is it still going on? Yes, according to Martin Cannon.

Interestingly, 'The Unabomber,' Ted Kaczynski, a mathematical genius who, from the 80's to the 90's, sent bombs to Universities and libraries, once attended Harvard as a student. It was while he was at college there that he participated in psychological experiments conducted by Dr Henry Murray, and according to many researchers, these were CIA sponsored MK Ultra experiments to test stress and attack a person's ego. Many have aligned these tests with the resulting actions carried out by Kaczynski, who killed three in his bombing campaign and injured many others.

What are the implications of this then? Given that it's college men who are the ones going missing, often being held for an extended period of time, and then placed dead in a stretch of water?

Of course, blaming the 'CIA, government, or military is perhaps again too easy an answer and it could be looking in entirely the wrong direction. There's just as much likelihood of it having absolutely nothing to do with nefarious secret aims of "the Government" and every possibility it could be an altogether different 'organization' entirely.

In fact, to demonstrate not only just how this could be possible and not within the bounds of outrageous conspiracy thinking, this exotic 'weaponry' was once highly sought after by another 'organization.'

Thomas Martinez and John Gunther's book, 'The Brotherhood of Murder,' published in 1984, covered the true story of a white supremacist Neo-Nazi group calling themselves 'The Order,' who some believed to have been responsible for the assassination of Jewish radio host Alan Berg, (though they were convicted of conspiracy not murder).

Back then, this white supremacist group had made contact with two government scientists who were engaged in clandestine research for the purposes of developing the ability to 'project chemical imbalances and render targeted individuals docile via certain frequencies of electronic waves.'

The authors, who belonged to this White supremacist group, claimed that for a price of $100,000, the two scientists were willing to make this available to the domestic terrorist group to use.

Some profilers behind these 'drowning' cases believe that we are looking at some form of domestic terrorist group again, although who they are and what their manifesto and purpose is, is not known.

Again however, it's not that simple…

Chapter 11:
Things Get Even Darker

Calling to mind the allegations made by some non-mainstream researchers that Sunil Tripathi was in some way used in the Boston Bombing, no matter how outlandish that sounds, there is also another altogether different theory about the fate of Sunil, as well as all that of the other young drowned men, and it gets even more disturbing.

It comes from a man called Christian White. What he says about Sunil is entirely different, and it's something that encompasses an explanation that is so dark. It's one of the most chilling things I've ever read, for it encompasses a world of the darkest magic and the most indescribable horror.

Of Sunil, Christian White says, "He willingly walked into the water."
Of all the victims, he says, "They are now entwined as one unified cog in the wheel of arcane rituals, thousands of years in the making."

Rituals for which he says "they did not choose to partake in. Rituals for which however, they were *Chosen*. They went into the water, and in their desolate waste, they were reborn."

"Once so vital, now.....grist for the mill. For a machine...A machine, full of teeth...they never saw coming."

Uncomfortably, this reminds me of Henry McCabe's horrific voicemail, with the sound of some kind of machinery in the background, as he screams and cries in pain and terror until a cold and detached voice tells him, "Stop it."

Why does Christian White say these things? What does he mean?

"It began," he says, "on October 7th, 2012, just around midnight. An email arrives in my inbox. Apparently from myself. All it said was,
"Psalm 139......from one WASP to another..."

(Does this mean the term 'White Anglo Saxon Protestant'? A term used to describe the preppy, upper class White proportion of society?)

Is he serious about actually receiving an email, from someone unknown? Saying, "From one WASP to another?" Is this a crucial clue about how these young men are being contacted, prior to their disappearances? Are people communicating with them before they drown or vanish? Or, is this some kind of joke? Or just artistic licence?
Psalm 139, abbreviated, says;
If I go up to the heavens, you are there;

if I make my bed in the depths, you are there.
If I settle on the far side of the sea,
even there your hand will guide me.'
It appears the Psalm refers not only to heaven but to the depths of the sea.

He continues, "One year later, literally at a molecular level, my life and very reality have changed; irrevocably."

His tone is fatalistic. "In life, there are decisions we choose to make, with free will, fully aware that they are decisions that can never be 'un-made'.... decisions that require inoculation against the human concepts of 'past' and 'future,' and I now live in permanent present. I am...infinitely blessed. In this "truth," I know that I will never look back. After all.....I simply can't."
What on earth does he mean?

Later, he will explain more about this. He describes himself as someone who is both an esoteric researcher, and a forensic internet expert, who uses this specialism to assist law enforcement with specially developed GIS based predictive mapping technology. He appears to have worked professionally as a forensic consultant, and investigator, at local and state level. He has also worked on paranormal TV shows.

However, what he writes about in regard to these cases, is far from easy to understand, as his story becomes both cryptic and highly sinister in tone, with the creeping sensation as one reads, that something harmful and evil is happening.

It appears that he too found himself perplexed and intrigued by the recurring theme of young men being found 'drowned.' He describes his own investigation into the death of Gregory Hart, which he says he spent a year looking into. This one happened in his town. Gregory was found drowned in the river in Providence, on February 14th, 2010.

As he begins to describe his investigation into the case, which he diarises on his *mindandmotives* blog, for some reason, as well posting photos of smiley faces taken from the graffiti he found, he also posts a map which shows geographical areas that have drug resistant T.B. (XDR T.B., a rare strain of Tuberculosis that is resistant to drug treatment). Why he does this is not explained, but it calls to mind the drug resistant outbreak of T.B. that was identified in the same area as where Elisa Lam was found, dead in the water Tower of the Cecil Hotel in Los Angeles, and it occurred at the same time that she was found. What is his implication here?

Continuing on, he focuses on the details of the particular drowning death in his town. The body was found "half-in and half-out" of the water, just like so many of the other young men. Gregory was an experienced swimmer and scuba diver. The medical examiner said that he'd been intoxicated. His blood alcohol was said to have been .25; a level consistent with the possibility of black-outs, double vision, and very poor motor skills. It was determined that he'd fallen into the River and drowned, which sounds perfectly reasonable; but his family don't understand this.

"You can't fall into this river. So I need to know what really happened," Greg's mother, Marianne said. "Somehow, he managed to tumble into a *fenced-off* river."

His family also pointed to the injuries he'd sustained; which were consistent with a violent attack. They said that he had broken bones in his face. Some will say that a fast flowing river can break bones, which it probably can, but that river wasn't fast flowing. The police told them that his phone had been in the water with him, but according to White, independent forensic examination showed that it had not been in the water, and that it had been tampered with; to the extent that the 'indicator' installed on his phone, as with all iphones, was scratched off to make sure it would not show it had not been in the water. The independent technical specialist said that these 'indicators' are installed on all iphones in order to prove if customers have negligently dropped their phones in water and thereby voided their warranty. Neither the independent expert nor the police technical experts were able to retrieve any information in the phone. The allegation was then that it had been deliberately tampered with so that no-one could see any information inside the phone with regards to the deceased man's activity on the phone prior to his death. What information was on that young man's phone, that *someone* didn't want it found? The family also believed that his body was not in the expected post-mortem condition; they did not believe the police when they said he had been in the water all the time he had been missing.

If, in Christian White's belief, this was a ritual, then why would it be that he was beaten? Well, I presume because the hierarchy and structure of this 'organization' expands on all levels and goes from the bottom to the top. It requires, for obvious practical reasons, to have 'boots on the ground.' It requires people to carry this out.

And now Christian says, "He is now no-where. No ghost, no afterlife. He is simply; gone. He became a symbol even by the time *he was drained.*"

Why is he saying that? As an esoteric expert, who will be described later in this book, pointed out to me, he may actually be playing with words and saying 'he is now here.'

He relates it to the graffiti he says was found; "The mysterious graffiti tag 'ANOK.' – 'Anochi' is the Divine 'I'; the Divine 'Self,' or 'Essence.' The ultimate context of Reality; Divine Existence. A Dark and Light Rituals. Ancient practices of vengeance and rebirth."

He continues, "Fire and smoke poured from the mountain....The thunder of awakening surged through each heart...a voice spoke out...."I am The Name, your God."

In its most simplistic explanation, rather than worshipping God as a divine and separate entity; 'Essence" is acknowledging the Self as The Divine above all else; 'I' as being part of GOD, in union with the Divine GOD.

Anochi is the Divine 'I;' the Divine Self. And this is about the search for Illumination through alchemy and ritual to achieve that status.

He says of 'Essence'; 'descriptive names do not apply, because even the concept of "Infinity" is by definition, a limitation. 'Essence' is beyond the finite and the Infinite.'

According to IYYUN, the centre for Jewish Spirituality, where Christian appears to have quoted from; When "Fire and smoke poured from the mountain....as the Divine Presence thrust them into profound revelation... a transcendent voice spoke out; "Anochi Ha-Shem Elokecha." 'Ha-Shem' is Infinity; that is, 'beyond' and transcendent.

For this reason, 'Essence' holds the key to resolving the existential tension between the *finite* and the *Infinite*. The 'I' is not only the 'I' of existence and form, but it is also the 'I' of 'no-thing,' the "'I' of 'infinite,' of wholeness and of emptiness.

Christian says, "With the revelation of Anochi, they experienced their own limited human existence and the unlimited Divine Existence in the absence of conflict. In this revelation, there was no duality, only Unity."
This is about the search for Illumination, through alchemy and ritual to achieve this desired state.

In the case of Sunil Tripathi, described earlier as an alleged possible 'body double' or 'patsy' in the Boston bombing, he disappeared on exactly the same day as Greg Hart, but 3 years later, and here White says, "I believe that, unlike Gregory, he *chose to go into the water, and* I believe this is taking place all over our world. Why? Alchemy; The marriage of two Rituals; "Trust" and "Love."

How does what he say make any sense? And yet, later, it will not appear as hard to understand. Interestingly, he adds, "The 'Smiley faces,' are not being left by the "killers." It's quite the opposite. They are created at the sites posthumously and purposefully. They are devices used as symbolic cleansing magick, attempting to counter the black, arcane and sacrificial ritualization. They are put there by Agents of great clarity and strength, in an effort of containing the psychic misfortune bestowed upon the place."

What he says next is very disturbing;

"Boys serve very specific purposes. The 'good' boys that earn their keep, until they outlive their usefulness, become responsible for the well-being of the girls they have come to know, *until they chose to slip into the cold ocean,* which due to their loyalty, will be of their own choosing; like a tribute."

Why would he say this? And who are the girls he refers to?

It gets worse;
'The naughty boys, well.....they go directly into the shallow water. And then, they are all gone...no ghost, no memories...as if they never ever lived in the first place. And then, "they" stay there. Awake and afraid and always always and forever and ever - underneath."

What again is he actually saying here? Is his imagination running wild? Is he talking in a purely 'creative' way only, or is he offering up much more information about how this is done than we could ever imagine? After all, the Professor and profilers I have spoken with are convinced that not only is this incredibly well organized, but girls too may play their part in this.

The chances are however, the most logical explanation here is that this is his way of expressing the idea he has as to who may be behind this. It is his creative way of 'painting the picture' for us; of giving us the scenarios he believes portrays what is being done and how it is being organized, surely? After all, he says he assists law enforcement professionally. Is he trying to say then, that this is the explanation of how their hierarchy is organized, from the ground up? Whatever it really means, his words make the blood run cold. He also describes himself as psychically intuitive; and having sought the advice of another person who too has this gift, it would appear that the most rational explanation here is the correct one. He is saying that he thinks he knows how and more importantly why this is happening.

Strangely however, he describes 'the girls' as though they are Spirits too. He calls them 'Akkadian girls who ruled all until G0D punished their pride with three hundred years of drought. The few who survived became Acadian; the keepers of the secret grail. They were punished again, and almost every one of them drowned "sent callously to 'the underneath'...awake, aware but NEVER EVER afraid...there, underneath, they simply wait..."

He says that 'somehow' some survived this second punishment too, and were "reborn." He says, "*She* has built into her canvas of 'reality' a very complex and very divine concept of an 'afterlife'. A place of boundless energy, a kingdom of black and whites. She and her shadow. Always together, never the same.'
So are the 'girls' in Spirit? Disembodied entities? Or is it a place? - Essence, the Divine Existence?

"For her i wander every night, from September to April, and always of two minds, with more happiness than I have ever known...and so, this is who "I" am. 'S/he' is the most dangerous...."

He/She? Two minds? What is going on? He isn't talking about real girls? These are bad, yet good Spirits? He is talking about himself then, and yet as a plural; as though he is possessed or now part of someone/something else. Of Essence? September to April is of course the time period when these 'drowning' cases happen.

The girls 'handler' he says, is "from the House of David."

Surely a biblical reference here, but what does it mean?

"He holds 'the quill' for safe keeping. At least 'they' let him think he does."

"Her station was once 'alec.'"

This is all very cryptic but the author, White, is clearly trying to say something. The only station that comes to mind is the CIA's Osama bin Laden tracking unit once code-named 'Alec Station.' Is he trying to say that the CIA is somehow behind this? It doesn't make any sense. Or again, is this some kind of art project mixed in with the drowning deaths; but why?

'Before that, it was as an internationally known "subversive."

Subversive groups are ones that exist to advocate the overthrow of governments, by force or violence.

Does this really tie in to the drownings? Why is he describing it in metaphysical and biblical terms, which makes it so difficult to understand?
In a very cryptic manner, he continues, explaining how he believes the 'drownings' are related to ancient immortals, archaic alchemy and metaphysical rituals.

He includes a link to a site describing 'junk' DNA called Alu. (And this reminds me of the links, albeit tenuous, that some of the boys had to both the Periodic Table of Elements, and Genetics and DNA, as mentioned at the beginning of the book)

'I am now a part of a family. Even when I have blood on my hands, this is nothing short of an honor. I am their wandering dog like in the days of Sumeria."
Blood on his hands? Is he saying he's a killer? Again, the most rational explanation is the correct one; He is not saying that his is killing or drowning these boys; he's saying that someone else is, but he thinks he knows how and more importantly why.

Is the motive behind all of this purely a religious one of some kind? Or, is it one of arcane and dark alchemy rituals, pursued for the purposes of reaching illumination through the deepest metaphysical concepts and practise?

When Christian White is talking of immortals, is he talking of beings on the astral plane rather then in real-life? Is the key to understanding this phenomenon related to that which can occur not in our everyday world, but on another plane altogether?

Perhaps this is the case, because not only this investigator, but also some of the victims are quite possibly looking outside of our dimension, into others. Who could be influencing these young men to look into these etheric and astral dimensions?

Perhaps one good example might be the case of Luke Helder, a young man who went in search of profound insights into the nature of our existence, and in pursuit of this illumination. It could of course alternately be said that Luke Helder was part of a college mind control indoctrination program; however, he most likely acted as he did, as a result of his own personal search for meaning and 'illumination.'

What perhaps for him began as the product of an innocent and inquiring mind, grew into a dark need for destruction as his search for enlightenment and oneness with the source, resulted in his mind getting taken over by malignant influences on the astral planes he sought to investigate and rise through.

Perhaps an ideal candidate for a black ops 'mind control' indoctrination; on the other hand, Luke Helder may have instead gone in way too deep on his esoteric journey and had not accounted for the darker forces that lurk within it, on the lower levels, just waiting to hijack a person's mind.

Luke was a student of Art at the University of Wisconsin, in 2002, and he would go on to create a 'smiley face map' across the Midwest, in a real-life project; one of planting pipe bombs in mailboxes. He was captured before he could complete the landscape map, but several people were seriously injured in the explosions.

(Interestingly, the first killings in the 'smiley face killers' theory also resulted in a smiley face map across the USA.)

When apprehended, Luke told the police that he had succeeded in dotting the two eyes of the map from successive bombs but was still working on completing the smile when he was captured.

His motives he said, ranged from wanting marijuana legalised, to wanting a change in the Government system to 'free people from enslavement.' The most interesting facet however, was his apparent complete obsession with immortality, astral projection, and esoteric study and practise.

Time magazine wrote in the aftermath, "Helder was a visionary, given to passionate harangues on immortality, astral projection and other esoterica." Class-mate, Amanda Dolan, was quoted as saying that she was impressed by his accounts of O.B.E.'s, (Out of body experiences.) "He said death is an illusion."

In a letter he wrote to his University Newspaper he said, "Whether it's meditation, channelling, or astral projection, all are ways of knowing."

He left extensive notes in rural post boxes, which described his 'Manifesto.' They said, "If you are under the impression that Death exists, you do anything to avoid it. I'm here to help you understand; you will live no matter what! It is up to you to open your minds. Few people understand death; There is no such thing as death! Religions were created to maintain the survival instinct. In fearing death, you conform. Mentally and physically; you create your own reality. The people I've dismissed from this reality are not at all dead. Conforming to the boundaries reduces the substance of your lives..."

Both law enforcement and his family however, were completely baffled by what the young man had been doing. Dennis Balaam, the Sheriff in Nevada where he was arrested after a police chase, described him as polite and respectful. "He shook my hand and called me sir."
Friends and neighbors where he grew up described him as "ordinary, quiet, regular."
But at college, things changed exponentially. According to an affidavit statement made to the F.B.I., his roommate James Devine said that Luke had told him, "Death is the way of going to another life." 'He said he is looking forward to it as a new experience.'

This reminds me of a remarkably similar message posted on facebook by Mason Cox, just hours before he died in a river.

'Not afraid of death cause I'm so curious of what's next.' The difference was, Mason Cox had never expressed an interest in Astral projection, or Out of Body Experiences, as far as we know.

It does however mirror what Christian White came to believe after his year long study into the cases of the drowning men. He too came to believe that life did not end after death. Instead, he believed that we continue in "a very divine concept of an afterlife; a place of boundless energy."

He says, "As the Ancients received the revelation of Anochi, they experienced the unlimited Divine Existence. Nothing exists outside of Essence. The process may simply be a matter of Revelation."

He continues, "The native Ojibwa used ON-O-KAY, meaning "working waters."

"Gregory went into the waters, And in his desolate waste he was reborn."

He is saying that Dying is to live; dying is to return to the original primordial Essence; where Perfection resides.

If when Christian White is talking of immortals, he is talking of Beings on the astral plane rather then in real-life, is the key to understanding these deaths related to that which can occur, not in our everyday world, but on another plane of existence altogether?

Again this reminds me of the person who contacted me, several years ago now, to warn me that when they had kept a blog tracking the deaths, they had suffered "extreme and severe astral and psychic attack" while looking into the deaths themselves, and that they now wanted nothing more to do with it. At the time, I took a look at the blog, and it was indeed covering the deaths, but I had no idea why someone would say they had come under psychic attack because of what they were doing. It unnerved me, and feeling freaked out by it, I didn't look at the blog again. It has since been deleted; and yet, perhaps this person was really onto something, something that others had never thought of, and certainly something that those doing it, did not want publicized.

When Mason Cox posted that message on his facebook page,
"Not afraid of dying cause excited as what's next."
A reply came quickly from 'someone' saying,
"This means something greater than expected."
Why would someone say that?
Is it just coincidence or synchronicity that several of the students, many studying philosophy and often described as 'deep' or 'critical' thinkers; such as Austin Hudson LaPore, and Jake Nawn, who will be described momentarily, were victim to a drowning death?

Had something not of this world infiltrated their lives? Are some of these victims having some kind of transcendental awakening? Or perhaps becoming involved in a group who are? Or, are they merely pawns in a game carried out by those already reconnected to the Essence?

Of course, nihilism is a philosophy that can be championed by many well-read and inquiring students, before they emerge into the working world and join the rest of society in the conventional progression into careers and conformity. That is not unusual at all, particularly at college, when studying poets and philosophers, and their minds being at an impressionable stage; but why does this theme of the world beyond our own, after-death, kept cropping up?

Mason Cox, who will be described shortly, was the epitome of the 'All-American boy,' and yet, just hours before he died he posted that message on facebook, "Not afraid of dying cause excited as what's next."

This to anyone who knew him, was wholly out of character, and indeed, some have even suggested that he did not write that message himself.

Toader Cazazu, who is missing wrote, "By the time you read this message I'll be sinking into the ocean ..."

Alchemy, the invisible world beyond us, immortality, survival of consciousness, transmutation of the soul and spirit. Certainly for Christian White, he has become, in his opinion, 'Essence.' He has completed his transcendence to 'perfection.' He too is no longer of this present world, he says.

To the literally '*uninitiated*' or 'unIlluminated' it's hard to understand all of this; however, while writing this book I was contacted by someone who was able to help me understand more clearly just what Christian was really talking about.
"He is talking about salvation through dark alchemy," explains Dan Mitchell of wellofhighstrangeness blog. Dan is a highly read esoteric & philosophical writer and an expert in esoteric illumination.

First though, I asked him what he made of the intriguing message I had found in a forum, mentioned at the beginning of this book;
"Just like the night good ol' Jack got two in one night and was almost caught- work unfinished. Alchemy? Transcendence of the soul/spirit/consciousness. My brother Germain has seen the hypocrisy, the pure greed and the lies conveyed at Nicea.
We take what we need and leave. Understand this: This is necessary. Life feeds on life feeds on life feeds on death feds on life. We will never leave, just sink back to where we came from. :)

Dan Mitchell believes that if this is a taunting message from the killers, they are "Taking the life energy of a murdered boy and absorbing that energy into their own consciousness, so that it becomes part of them, strengthens them, feeds them. Basically, by murdering someone, you can take their emotive energy and apply it to your own conscious development. This is their magnum opus; to become living Gods through alchemical ritual murder. So that is the context of their alchemy. It is murder."

Dan says, "He seems to be saying that he is carrying out this work, but he has run into a "slight problem." He seems to be hinting perhaps that he had almost been caught. When he says, "We take what we need and leave," it sounds as if they do the deed and leave. He is being obvious that this is a group of people, not just one man. Most disturbing in the excerpt, at least to me, was his saying, "We will never leave, just sink back to where we came from." I don't think he/they are referring to themselves dying and returning to God. His writing is only slightly ambiguous. What he is saying is that if things get too hot, or if there is too much scrutiny on them, they don't stop doing what they are doing, they just go back to whatever mundane vocation they may have and take a break from their alchemical magnum opus of becoming living gods. To me the language is unmistakable."

"His reference to Nicea is simply the council of Nicea. Many believe that the council of Nicea essentially determined the Christian religious cannon and the orthodox beliefs of the Christian church. What this man is saying is that the Christian church and it leadership is full of lies and greed. He believes that salvation is through a kind of dark alchemy. He is not an Orthodox Christian. Nicea was about solving the Arian Heresy and determining the proper calendar for Holy Days, it really wasn't about determining the verities of Christian Faith."

Of course, here perhaps it should be recalled the earlier mention of 'Baptism by Torture' which according to William Schweiker, of the University of Chicago, 'had been done at least since the time of St Augustine, stemming from the Council of Nicea. Practices similar to waterboarding developed as a way to torture heretics; this torture was meant to bring 'salvation' to these heretics. It could be justified as an act of mercy, even when done in lethal form, and it was meant as an act to keep the sinner from continuing to sin, and the choice offered in this 'baptism by torture' was either repentance of heresy or death by drowning.'

When Dan Mitchell contacted me, it was because he has also followed some of these 'drowning' cases himself, and has written about the phenomenon of the missing and drowned on his blog 'wellofhighstrangeness.' He has given me permission to include some of his own thoughts here about what could be happening. In his opinion, not only are we dealing with very much a human element in these cases, but also it appears, there are even darker things too, things that have always been there; it's just that we can't see them. Sometimes maybe we sense them, but most of the time they are there without any awareness from us, and their power is all pervading.

Dan has a take on what is causing these drownings, and as well as the hand of humans potentially behind it, the 'others' behind these 'ritual murders' tie in with the possibility of communication with higher entities. It again makes for very disturbing reading.

"There is a deception at work that goes deep. So deep in fact that one cannot fully escape it as long as they are encased in an earthen vessel," says Dan, and what he says next, is simply horrifying;

"Nobody understands the sinister nature of the world they are living in; a world where people are being hijacked and murdered because they are living on a relatively low point of a cosmic food chain. Make no mistake; this is a major cover up. No-one will speculate on it, but if people knew the depth of this, they would be terrified to be outside at night, whether out in the country or in the city. There aren't just hundreds of cases of missing people found in or by bodies of water, there are tens of thousands. I've been obsessed with missing people most of my life; particularly where the seemingly normal people who suddenly simply lost their minds, travelled barefoot out into the middle of nowhere, and died. Most of the time they are found missing their shoes. Most times they are found in or beside bodies of water."

"The majority don't understand we are living on a machine that is controlled by an intelligence; a Hive mind, that at any moment is capable of hijacking people. The physical world is something like a terrarium. (A Terrarium is a sealed glass container, often used for example to house plants.) This terrarium is under the control of a Hive mind that has human proxies operating throughout, in both low and high positions. The purpose of the terrarium is to harvest a certain type of energy that is given off by people.

When Dan refers to the Hive mind, it reminds me of what Christian said; that he received an email "Apparently from myself, which says, "From one Wasp to another. Psalm 139....'If I settle on the far side of the sea, even there your hand will guide me.'

Was that from one of the 'human proxies' of the Machine? A 'proxy,' meaning that which represents someone or *something* else.

"People are controlled by this Hive mind, which essentially controls the terrarium. The world exists under a type of grid pattern. These are not ley lines. Each square in the grid is controlled by a spirit or intelligence; a Genius Loci, that has control over that particular area. It is a multi-layered, multi-dimensional control system that extends from the seen to the unseen. This is an ancient concept. These beings are parasites; archonic, sinister and ignoble intelligences."

"The Enochian Angels of John Dee were Loci parasites." (Dr John Dee was a conjurer, scryer and seer during Queen Elizabeth's reign in the 17th century, in England, who believed he was communing with Angels.) The Genius Loci only gain power from the energies given off by 'Aryans.' (Aryans being in its most simplistic and mundane terms, Caucasians.) They will target non-Caucasians too however, he says, if no Caucasians are available. "Aryan People are being taken because they produce the highest amount of this "energy" that feeds the machine reality. That these are young people, good looking, and bright, reveals the high amount of energy they possess.

"I am not convinced in the least that the GHB found in their system is from spiked drinks as much as it is being naturally produced by the body when it is interacting with the subtle energy of demons. Sleep paralysis and GHB are linked. You can't have one without the other. It is well known that sleep paralysis and demonic intrusion are also linked."

"This Machine (and its underlings) turns victims into "Luna-tics" who make strange phone calls to family members or the police, before they vanish. These phone calls are often non-sensical and reveal that their minds have become confused, scrambled and, unable to tell where they are or what is happening to them."

He sums up the potential scenario very well, "There is a nightmarish quality to the few remaining hours of their lives."

"I'm intensely psychic and have communicated with people no longer of this world. It has taken a heavy toll on me but it's given me profound insights to things that happen beyond our domain."

Why is it always that these people are found in or near water?
Dan's answer is horrific, "Water is like electricity inside the machine. When a person is hijacked by the Loci, their corpse will almost always be found in water in what appears to be a drowning. Once the body is submerged, it will unleash its terror into the water like a slaughtered animal releases its karma into the meat that is consumed."

Interestingly, he points out the same commonality as Professor Gilbertson and Ret'd Kevin Gannon originally did when they were studying the early cases; "Many disappearances will occur during waxing phase of the moon. The moon is a transmitter; everything functions like a machine. In the early days of alchemy, the astronomical signs of the planets were also used as alchemical symbols."

"People are becoming willing sacrifices to the dark power that is behind these disappearances. People are being taken, their minds hijacked by something very powerful that convinces them to sacrifice their own lives. These are likely the Genius Loci of a specific area, which are extremely powerful *disembodied* intelligences. However, there are still humans hand at work in some of these disappearances. But it all works toward the same end, human 'tributes' are energy that is put into the machine to power it."

Or as Christian White said, 'grist for the mill. For a machine full of teeth...a machine he never saw coming.'

"Each Loci has underlings, which are none other than the classical demons. These demons are fully able to hijack a human mind, confuse it, and kill it by deception. Demons can manifest physically, but they cannot retain physical form for very long. The disassociated accounts of being chased and followed by shadowy people is the hallmark of demonic intrusion into reality. I have witnessed this."

"While this warning may appear extreme, it should be understood that dark and intrusive currents at work in the physical domain have extreme power and control. The demiurge," (in Gnosticism, a being subordinate to the Supreme Being and a controller of this material world of ours, which opposes everything which is not spiritual) "is a vast intelligence that is spread across the earth. It is more of a machine than an actual entity. It gives its commands to the various Loci, who in turn download that information into all types of embodied and disembodied intelligences which operate in the physical domain as well as the subtle. It has physical and non-physical agents."

"I would be curious to know what they were reading or studying outside of their college studies, if anything. This is an important detail for me personally because I believe that the mind can be tuned by certain types of ideas. If the mind is tuned just right, it can be hijacked much easier. From my own research, I found that Kayelyn Louder (a young woman who was also found dead in a creek, and who Dan predicted would be found in water, dead.) was into Jungian psychology, serial killers, and various spiritualities....these are things I found on her Facebook page before she had been found."

"Practices aimed at "astral endeavours" are dangerous; disembodied intelligences live within the mind space. I have watched many 'seekers' destroy themselves over the years, some even to death."

(This appears to tie in with the things I have mentioned with regards to the young men leaving cryptic messages on their facebook or twitter, and of making terrified phone calls just before they disappear.)
"Not afraid of death,"
"If I'm found dead...it wasn't suicide."
"This means something greater than expected."

Dan continues, "I have always viewed this phenomenon as something sinister. I think there are human agents and non-human agents involved. For the victims, sometimes it may be that a very strange or obsessive thought overtakes them. Many serial killers or spree killers have admitted the same. The obsessive thought is often so intense that it might induce panic causing a fight or flight reaction to take place. Many of the victims are likely fleeing without really thinking about where they are going."

"The rational centres of the mind are likely taken over by this point and the person is really just confused and witnessing their own seemingly incoherent behavior. This is just hypothetical on my part, but I base it on my own interactions with these things over the years. They are exceedingly nasty and dangerous. Often times even thinking about them can draw them in. These are things I'm sure you are already clearly aware of."

And now we get to Alchemy again, which at the beginning of this book was the introductory theme, and now is what appears could possibly be an of the overriding theme in these deaths..
One boy said, "Look under the Periodic Table for the answer."
Another boy was found near graffiti which said "H3yme", "Why me?" Hydrogen, Trituim...and H20; Water.

Alchemy; a credo, a dogma, a belief. Something which as its motivation, could lie in the realms of the darkest underworld and yet in the search for the highest 'Divine

Source;' a search for transcendence of the soul, a search for salvation through 'illumination.'

The aims of the Alchemists was to find the Stone of Knowledge; the 'Philosopher's Stone;' but not in a literal meaning; more in a symbolic meaning, of searching for the elixir of Immortality, Eternal life, of Perfected Man as a Divine Living God.

But, more than this, it is also a battle; a war fought against the archonic entities which both inhabit and seek to invade.

Says Dan Mitchell, "True alchemy is about exiting the machine/demonic system we are trapped in as human beings. This goes so much deeper than most people would be willing to realize. In my own experience, many people cannot handle the eerie nature of it all. There is something very disturbing about it. It simply haunts you. Of Magic, from Goetia (the 17th Lesser Key of Solomon and such tomes which existed to summon Angels and Demons) to Aleicester Crowley, the magicians' sole power is used for attempting to appease these parasitic intelligences that have dominion over our land, and sea."

Chillingly, he says, "The only defence is the work of self-cultivation and perfection; of becoming the divine being;"

In other words, only Alchemical ritual workings of the highest and most profound level & the achieving of 'illumination,' can serve as defence and protection against these archonic intelligences.

He refers specifically to the practice of Theurgy; this being the practice of magical rituals to invoke the Gods with the intention of reaching GOD, and uniting with the divine; of achieving Henosis; Henosis being a mystical 'oneness' and perfection of oneself.

The term Theurgy refers back to the time of the mid-second-century neo-Platonist work, The Chaldean Oracles, where our earthly matter is considered a dense region from which the enlightened soul must emerge as it sheds its body, on its path upward toward the Father, the Highest God. Through the correct rituals and conduct, it is believed that the soul can be freed from the limitations of matter, freed of its existence on this earthly plane, and can then better defend itself from the demonic who lurk in the lower realms between mortals and God.

Theurgy is a series of rituals and operations performed with the objective of recovering the transcendent 'Essence' by retracing the divine 'signatures' through the layers of Being. From the material matter of our existence, to the etheric. In Platonism the goal of Henosis is to achieve union with *The Source*, or *The Essence*. The highest stage of deification is 'tabula rasa' or a 'blank state,' where the person is then able to merge with *The Source*.

Achieving this, the person is then dissolved, and completely re-absorbed back into the monad; that which is above the demiurge.

This is why Christian White talks of Gregory Hart, one of the young men found half-in half-out of the water, as
"He is no-where. No ghost, no afterlife. He is simply; gone. He became a symbol even by the time *he was drained.*"
He has been reabsorbed. And yet he is 'Now Here.'

The theurgist works 'like with like': at the material level, he works with physical symbols; at the higher level, it is done so by mental and spiritual practices. The ultimate goal is to reach the level where the soul's inner divine can merge with The Divine Source. The individual is reabsorbed back into the primordial from which all things came, and at the point of unity id returned to source. They are changed form a being of energy, to coalesce with the infinite 'potential,' their 'person' is now gone, and they are rejoined with the Essence, the Source and are now infinite, never ending 'potential.' The Chaldean philosophy is that by falling to earth, man's soul had sunk, and so he must climb back up to the Source, through the use of the Cosmos, Ritual and Magic. He must use Ritual and magic to achieve Illumination that will lead his soul back to its divine origins.

This of course, is a layman's explanation; my own, and others are far better at providing a more comprehensive and expert explanation. Dan Mitchell calls this state, "A deathless individuality, an individual expression of the GOD, the Deus Absconditus, in the glorious Hyperborea. This world, which some of us call Thule, Hyperborea, or Arcadia, is populated by Shepherds with a most terrible yet glorious visage."

"Terrible in that to see them is to see ones death. Glorious in that once they are seen, their luminous presence can never be forgotten nor likened to any mortal glory. These beings, beyond the threshold of death, partake in the eternal sacrament of primordial freedom."

"They are divine God-Men, people who were once humans, who endured the great suffering and loss the initiatory path demands."

"Matter simply is not present at this most fundamental level. In its place is nothing but empty space. There is nothing but pure, empty freedom."

Is this then perhaps, a motivation for a few of the victims themselves; a very personal and esoteric search for illumination. More importantly however, what it most certainly could be, is the very motivation behind those who are the 'human agents' of the Hive mind-machine in which we all reside.

Dan continues his explanation about what it is that we are up against, when out alone on a dark night, when some fall victim to this nefarious discarnate predatory machine.

"Without an initiatory understanding of the unseen world, one can never truly understand the subtle mechanisms at work in this one; an occult war that has been raging for many ages. Most people don't understand that the real technology behind this war is magic. I am not referring to Crowley or the modern Chaos magic; these are nothing more than base thaumaturgy and will employ just servitor-type entities who are merely the underlings of the Loci."

In other words, he is saying that low magic will not reach these higher entities we are up against; it will not affect nor destroy them. It will only connect with their underlings, who will turn it against us, and the impact of this low magic when trying to use it as a weapon against 'the machine' will of be little impact; its effectiveness will be negligible against the real force and power. Those we are up against, the higher level human agents of the Hive mind, are using magic of the most powerful against us.

"I'm talking about the real kind of magic; not the magic that's written in books, but that which is handed down through generations among the influential families of 'our enemy.'"

We are, he believes, up against a very arcane and highly powerful form of black magic and alchemical ritual. We are no match for this.

"It is black magic indeed; and make no mistake; this deception runs deep. Specifically, I am referring to mind control, and the alchemical transmutation of lead to gold (money magic)."

Chillingly, he also refers here to ritual human sacrifice.

"Each of these feeds a certain layer of the machine."

It would seem that to really understand these concepts, and particularly the reason why one would involve themselves in this offering of human 'tributes' to the machine, one would need to be on the path of practising the magnum Opus oneself, with much learning of Alchemy and Symbolism, Hermeticism, Gnosis, Kabbalah, Ancient Philosophies, and more.

Robert Ambelain, esoterist writer from the Masonic Scottish Rite, described information received from 'a Rosicrucian group in Cairo' which having been translated, appears to explain one interpretation of the process of transmutation and initiation;

'The initiate of the Great Work will have met strange companions along the way: the Archons who stand watch over the thresholds of the intermediary worlds, to bar the way to the seeker, and symbolic personalities; the Swan and the Crow, the Lion and the

Dragon, and so on.... each of which pose their own enigma for him to solve.'

'It is only after having understood their secret meanings that the pilgrim will finally see the Star of Compostella, which announces the end of the golden periplus. Life will eventually deliver one of its greatest secrets to him. Now transmuted by this second Revelation, the Initiate finally becomes the Adept, and, in the inner plane alone, with the Arcana finally conquered, he can finally become transformed, to become and remain forever: the Illuminated One.'

'The Illuminated One, in his turn, transmits his own spiritual light to those who, intelligent and docile prima materia, will themselves *accept the need to die as lead in order to be reborn.*'

If understanding the alchemical illumination process is a little difficult, to an 'uninitiated' person such as myself, perhaps an alternate explanation makes the concept of immortality easier to grasp.
Bestselling science writer Robert Lanza coined the term 'Biocentrism.
"Albert Einstein, after the death of a very good friend of his said, "He has departed from this strange world ahead of me. That means nothing. People like us.....know that the distinction between past, present and future is only a persistent illusion."

Lanza says, "Evidence now suggests continually that Einstein was correct; death is an illusion. Our classic way of thinking was an objective independent observer; but experiments now show it's the opposite. Because we associate ourselves with our body, and our body dies, we believe in death, but biocentrism tells us we are not just carbon and molecules. If you add *consciousness, it becomes clear why time and space and even matter itself depend on the observer, (us.) Space and time are simply tools of our mind. Death doesn't exist in a timeless, spaceless world. Immortality doesn't mean a perpetual existence in time, but resides outside of time itself.*

Lynne McTaggart in her findings in 'The Field; The Quest for the secret force of the Universe,' discovered that significant numbers of scientists were coming together to establish scientific proof of an 'Energy Field,' that everything in the universe was interconnected by waves, spread out through time and space that tied everything to each other.

The basic most fundamental laws of physics state that energy cannot be destroyed; it is infinite. It cannot be destroyed, but it can be converted to different form. 'Quantum physicists discovered that matter was completely indivisible. The Universe could now only be understood as a dynamic web of interconnectedness. Indeed, time and space themselves appeared now to be just arbitrary constructions.'

'There now appeared to be scientific validation for a model of consciousness that was not limited to the body but was an ethereal presence- an idea which had largely been the domain of religion, mysticism and new age spiritualism.'

A group of scientists, including two astrophysicists have been conducting experiments and solving complex equations that they believe even furnish irrefutable proof of human survival of bodily death. Michael Roll, who heads *The Campaign for Philosophical Freedom*, is the spokesman for the group. R. D Pearson, one of Roll's colleagues, a former University lecturer whose specialty is thermodynamics and fluid mechanics, has written a book called *Intelligence behind the Universe,* in which put simply, he claims it contains mathematical proof to explain the cosmic force that drives the phenomenon of continuing life. Pearson et al see post-mortem survival humans as just part of a multi-dimensional sub-atomic matrix, on which all 'forms' of life exits. In this model, physical materialisations are but the temporary merging of different frequencies, from two separate levels of the unifying 'grid.'

Are these above accounts, findings, and statements validation of the possibility that a very real 'invisible' realm exists very closely to our own and it is from here that entities or unfamiliar creatures can emerge, just as we ourselves will one day enter another 'state' and dimension?

Life transcends our linear way of thinking. When we die, in the inescapable matrix, we simply return, in this non-linear dimensionality, and ancient esoteric knowledge has known this for millennia. Dan Mitchell for one, says he has seen them in their own dimension.

Is this really what these young men are up against?
"A world where people are being hijacked and murdered because they are living on a relatively low point of a cosmic food chain. Make no mistake; this is a major cover up. If people knew the depth of this, they would be terrified to be outside at night, whether out in the country or in the city. There aren't just hundreds of cases of missing people found in or by bodies of water, there are tens of thousands."

When it comes to the way in which some of these young men have panicked, run in fear for their lives, calling friends, family or the police in terror, and then inevitably been found some time later, floating in water, makes one wonder if Dan Mitchell is right. In particular, the human element at play here, as a servitor of the greater archonic controller; stalking the young men, drugging them and drowning them as an arcane offering to the demiurge, or through the use of mind control, even prompting them to drown themselves, to offer them up to their Lord and Master as a 'blood sacrifice,' in their own quest for immortality and illumination. It's the most chilling and harrowing thought.

Their offerings to the machine, to energize and feed it as they feed too their own consciousness, is of the 'best;' the young, the fittest, the most intelligent, and the most promising young men, full of potential and energy.

Others have suggested that this goes even further; that they are offered up as sacrifice for another purpose; that of taking out the next generation of potential influencers and leaders. It's probably important to note that a lot of the young men were inspirational, were interested in philosophy, politics, and other academic subjects which are of crucial importance as our race progresses; biochemistry, advanced engineering, for example.

One avid researcher pointed out to me the case of Jake Nawn, who was found dead in the water on November 12th, 2015. Is it possible that within the tragic case of Jake there is an esoteric angle? Could Jake have been unwillingly and unknowingly led down a path of no return?

He was a very well liked 23 year old student at Plymouth State University. He loved poetry and music. He had lots of friends. He disappeared on Thursday 12th November and was found 5 days later in the river. His friends thought he might be hiding out in the woods for an unknown reason and they took his favourite books into the woods with notes written inside of them and placed them around the areas he most liked to hike, hoping he would be drawn to them.

The search began for Jake only a few hours after he failed to show up to meet his family at a restaurant in town. He had told his Mom that from 2pm to 3.15pm he was going to class and then he would meet them at the restaurant at 4 pm. The police were reported to have begun searching for him as soon as his family reported his absence, because according to his Mom, the previous weekend he had been hospitalised briefly due to a mental health issue.

Every day that he was missing, hundreds of people went out searching the woods for him. It was to be five days until a group out walking saw his body in the water of the Pemigewasset River. His autopsy determined that he had drowned, although crucially the coroner said, "The exact manner of death will remain undetermined."

Jake Nawn took writing courses with lecturer Ethan Paquin, who said of the student, "He was well-read for his age. Some of his poetry was dark, but also playful. It was E.E. Cummings-esque. He had a willingness to experiment and take risks. He waxed philosophically. He was a thoughtful, gentle soul."
One of E. E. Cummings poems is called 'I will wade out.'
'I will wade out.... Alive with closed eyes. to dash against darkness......I will rise.. After a thousand years.

Researcher, Jim C. Smith, who has been following these cases for a while now too, pointed out something to me that the young man had put on his Facebook page, ten days before the tragedy. On November 2nd he had posted a video. Given the young man's enjoyment of poetry and experimenting with it, and with his favourite authors said to include the avant guarde Charles Bukowski, there's every chance that this researcher and now myself are reading for too much into what is in actual fact a pastiche or a satire.

The video he made has been liked and commented on by many friends and so the likelihood is that we are seeing it from a different perspective than his friends did. Chances are it's just a joke. However, could it possibly be interpreted as holding clues? Was he revealing a message hidden within it? Coming from the view point that someone is killing young college men in water, and now he too is dead in water, maybe it could.

The video shows him on the screen, talking to an unknown person, on the phone or maybe skype, with an earphone in one ear. You don't hear or see the other person. You just see Jake's his head and upper body.
He says,
 "The hard part is when you try to mix that with everything else and then it just dies. Because there's

rain when....no, no, no." (He is vehemently disagreeing with the other person.)

"Yeah 'cos when you start talking philosophy like that I just really cannot go with you in it. It's far too upsetting. Far too unknown.....You know how it went down..."

The scene cuts to a garage, to what looks like people in there, perhaps having a party...It cuts to a street view; again, this could have an entirely different meaning to him and his friends, however, he continues, "I'm sweeping up it all, beyond any reasonable doubt. Happy???" He asks, strongly emphasising the word and staring close up into the laptop screen.

Here, despite it being disregarded as not true and just an urban legend, having liaised with those who conducted the original investigations, they stick by their allegations that smiley face graffiti was invariably found.

Jake continues, talking about a totally unrelated topic. Again is it some kind of in-joke? It's very possible.

Then, "Yeah kid u speak good things, I could go on but ...Yeah, I thought it was a gold rush, yeah I did."

Cut again,

He says, "Don't let them know you're fake"/or "what you think.")

Cuts to Outside, a roof top onto the street.

"You're gonna b ok? Yeah, when u really look into the mystery and the place and the settings and the symbolism, you're f...d, yeah ....."

How is this video in any way a clue? It may not be, but some of the words he used are very interesting. Is this a message within a message?

His words include, 'dies, rain, gold, philosophy...It's far too upsetting... Far too unknown. You know how it went down. Happy??? I thought it was a gold rush. Don't let them know what you think. When you look into the mystery, the place, the settings, the symbolism, you're f...d.."

'The mystery, the place, the settings, the symbolism...'
What or where is he describing?
Did he know something? Did he know too much?
Is he talking about some kind of organization? Did he unwittingly and innocently become naively sucked into something and get in way over his head; was he then unable to extricate himself when he realized?
What happened to him that resulted in him having to be admitted for a short time for mental health difficulties just a few days prior to this?

Many will call this 'guesswork' and it is not the intention to upset the family with insensitive suppositions here. Coming from the angle I am looking from however, it's interesting to note the reference to Philosophy, and Gold; is this the Periodic Table again, and alchemy? Gold in alchemy represented the perfection of all matter on any level, including the mind, spirit, and soul. Philosophers believed that man's body is a microcosm of the Universe, and as such, bodily fluids, like the Universe, should contain Gold. The Philosopher's stone was not only considered to be a physical material but also a symbol perfection and immortality. Gold is one of the seven metals of alchemy (gold, silver, mercury, copper, lead, iron and tin). For the alchemist, it represented the perfection of all matter on any level, including that of the mind, spirit, and soul.

Is this all conjecture that is now biased towards trying to find the answer and looking for clues that fit the answer wanted? Like others who firmly believe that the real clues lie in the names of the boys and the places in which they disappeared or were found dead?
In Duluth, New York State, in 2004, two boys disappeared in quick succession. On October 10th, Grant Geiselhart is found dead. That same day Nathan Williams, whose nickname was "Fish," was scheduled to return from his fishing trip in the same area. Later he too is found dead. Nearby, these words are allegedly found close to Grant Geiselhart's place of death;
'Flow on with the Fishes. GOD Grants Pure Wishes,'
Both of the boy's names appear to some extent within this message.
It's very possible, and open to debate of course, that we are all wrong. If nothing else, perhaps it at least provides food for thought.

Does what Jake said tie in with that taunting message found in a forum discussing the cases? The one from the Japanese i.p.?

'Just like the night good ol' Jack got two in one night and was almost caught- work unfinished. Alchemy? Transcendence of the soul/spirit/consciousness. My brother Germain has seen the hypocrisy, the pure greed and the lies conveyed at Nicea. We take what we need and leave. Understand this: This is necessary….'

There were many theories about who Jack the Ripper was, including a surgeon to the Queen, and a famous artist, while others say the murders were 'Masonic' occult ritual deaths.

If 'brother Germain' is a reference to the Count de St Germaine, then he was thought either to have been a grand fake, or an Ascended master who never died and remained eternal, appearing in various centuries throughout history, before taking himself off from the European cities in which he was given lodgings by the Kings, to Shambala; only to apparently return in more recent times to Mount Shasta. In all of his sightings, he never aged.

Diaries from several famous historical figures, including Catherine the Great and Casanova, described him. Madame de Pompadour, the aging mistress of the French King, supposedly saw him at a dinner party in Paris in 1760. He looked familiar to her yet this was what confused her; she was certain she had met the same man half a century earlier in Venice; yet he looked exactly the same now. He had not aged in any way, despite it being fifty years later.

Strangely, it was often recorded by his friends and acquaintances that he never appeared to eat any food. He would hint at having been present during the building of the Pyramids, and he spoke with intimate knowledge as though he had been present at things which had happened hundreds of years before his present time, including the time of Jesus. He also made claims that he had been present at the Council of Nicea in 325 A.D.

Not only was he a Rosicrucian, he was a Freemason, and had spent time in the Far East where he had become an initiate to Fraternities there who studied Rosicrucian and Hermetic science and the 'The Philosopher's stone.' In fact, he was also associated Knights Templar.

In 1938, Theosophy magazine wrote of him, "How many realized they were conversing with an emissary of that Great Fraternity of Perfected Men."

He was documented as having been a learned alchemist, who had been tutored by masters of the Mystery Schools in the Orient, where he was schooled in esoteric knowledge. Once in Europe, he was funded by Kings and had his own alchemy laboratories within their walls. He was also a member of secret societies.

It was said that he was Immortal and eternal, like the Philosopher's stone, and that he had achieved Illumination. Some says he was an ascended master, others that he came from the ancient Lemurian race.

Alternately, he may even have been a time-traveler, according to a letter he sent to Voltaire, the great French philosopher....

Neo Barnabus Maximus said to look under the Periodic Table for the answer too. Does this have something to do with alchemy? Or is it about life-expansion, genetics, DNA, or even time travel experimentation?

Interestingly, as I was finishing writing this book, I received another email from someone who had also heard me talking on a radio show about these cases.
It reads; "Whatever's going on needs funding and organizing....and a religious type fervor to carry on carrying on with it. I think a pagan off-shoot of misguided Caucasians, might be behind the drownings. A little hard to explain what's real or magic in someone's mind. God likes to give people enough rope to hang themselves if they wanna turn their back on him. Satanists?.... and there's many levels of those...from idiot Caucasian ones into death metal music, to the occultists, to the kabbalists.'

'However, it always made me wonder how THEY could ever let "AREA 51" technology go...unused or abused by them. I know that sounds "way out"...but just a logical conclusion to me..... I think it is our own Atlantian Technology, dug up...and now used...to abuse us mentally/physically.'

'I think the ones at the top, hop in a "UFO" and cloak it and go "hunting" in wilderness areas, that are OWNED by them via the UN's world heritage organization, thereby taking the land from underneath us, until we are just squatters.... I'd say they got their grip on all our Adamic Exotic Technology.'

Chapter 12:
Not Afraid of Death

Does anything described so far, help to explain why Mason Cox wrote this on his timeline on facebook, just hours before he ended up dead in water.
"Not afraid of death cause I'm so curious of what's next.'

This was the last post on Mason Cox's facebook page. A week later, his body was found in a river, along with that of his best friend. It was classified as 'accidental drownings.' Both autopsies determined that they had died from "accidental drowning compounded by hypothermia," according to Sherry Lang, spokeswoman for the Georgia Medical Examiner.

They both lived in Gainesville, Georgia and the boys had gone out around 3 a.m. on New Year's Day to do some night fishing. Just prior to this, Mason had posted his message on facebook. His facebook page is still up, as is his Mother's facebook page calling for Justice for her son.

On his facebook page, the messages prior to this post, over the days before he went missing, were not of this ilk. They were positive and inspiring messages to live every day the best you could, to train and keep fit and to eat healthy. Very different to his last message, just hours before he was to die.

Why did he write that message? Was it merely a youthful expression with very little deeper meaning? Everyone at that age thinks they can cheat death; that it will never happen to them. It's common for youths to read Nietzsche or Baudelaire, for example, and to enjoy maudlin writings and sentiments. Mason Cox however, was a typical 'all American Boy.' He posted about fitness, about inspiring people, about living well and eating well. He was only 20 years old. He had expressed no previous thoughts about dying or life after death. Or was there something going on behind the scenes, that those close to him did not know about?

A friend replied to his post, saying, "This means something greater than expected."
What did his 'friend' mean? It's impossible to know; because the post was deleted some time later; the 'friend' now untraceable.

Mason's mother said, after he failed to come home from fishing, "My son left his phone and wallet in his room. He's just gone."
The police had been looking for the two missing boys for a week before they were found, despite them only having gone to a neighbor's dock to fish there. The search teams had used sonar to search the water, although it had frozen over so they had to break holes in the ice to do so. Even so, the curious thing is that despite the intensive search, their bodies weren't found

in the water where they were known to have gone that night.

Mason had left his phone behind that night. David had taken his. The police said the battery 'ran out;' others would say it was switched off, at around 6 a.m. It would not be too much of a stretch of the imagination to suggest that it was not David who turned his phone off.
Mason's mother says, "In police reports neighbors heard screaming for help around 5.30am."

This would then make it potentially more difficult for someone to turn their own phone off after something had happened to them; especially after death. The likelihood is that both boys were dead by 6 a.m. The last cell phone signal from his phone came from the area they were fishing in, at 5:47 a.m.

Mason's mother is among others who are fighting to have the official investigation re-opened. She has several reasons for wanting this. Having studied the autopsy photos and having seen her son after he died, she points out;
"My son was beaten, teeth missing, blunt trauma to the back of his head. His eye so horrible... His stomach black and blue."

Dawson County Sheriff's Office however reported that "neither body exhibited evidence of internal or external trauma."

During her long fight for the investigators to listen to her, she has heard various rumors from local people, one of which is blood-curdling;
"Something about a cartel out of Gainesville. Beat up my son, and at gunpoint they were made to tread ice cold water until they drowned. Even in police reports neighbors heard someone screaming for help around 5.30am."

Mason's jacket was never found. Oddly, they didn't appear to have taken their fishing gear with them. It was found in their bedrooms. Were they meeting someone?

Mason's mother is seeking justice for her son. The police she says, so far, have refused to re-open the case. After he went missing, his mother said that she received calls of alarm from his friends who had spotted his facebook post; they couldn't understand why he would write about death. He was going to be a fire-fighter, and he had, according to his Mom, given her a birthday present only recently; "by accepting Jesus Christ as his personal savior. Before he was found, she said, "He is a major swimmer. He's very strong. He could swim the ocean like crazy. He didn't just fall into the lake and drown."

People looking into the case have suggested that the last facebook post was not written by Mason himself. They think it could have been written by his killer(s) as a taunting message. The thing is it does appear to have

been posted to facebook before he left his house, if the timelines are correct, although it was in the early hours of the morning so perhaps people were not so aware of the exact time? Others say he had already left the house at this point. The suggestion is then, that the same people who turned off David's phone also sent the cryptic message on David's facebook. What I find more curious however, is that over the course of time, there have been two different people replying to this facebook post. In response to his message,
'Not afraid of death cause I'm so curious of what's next,'
A person replies,
'This means something greater than expected.'
Again, it's very cryptic and the meaning is not easily understood. It could be purely mundane in its meaning. On the other hand, what I find very strange is that this message was posted by one person, who was then replaced by another person. So, in other words, a person called Daniel posted that reply. Then, at some point in time this person was replaced by a person called Leinad, who posted the exact same message. Now, either that person simply changed their name, for some bizarre reason, or two people posted the exact same message at different time periods, with the first person deleting their comment and it being replicated and posted by another, different person. The reply was exactly the same words;
'This means something greater than expected.'

Is this a strange but meaningless anomaly, or does it point to something more sinister? Both messages have now gone from his facebook page. Why have they disappeared? Were they friends of his, replying to a perfectly innocuous post? Or, were they strangers? Were they his killers?

According to Eau Claire News,
"Rescue crews pull man from Half Moon Lake, brought to hospital."
On February 23^{rd,} in 2010, a young man was taken to hospital after he was rescued from the banks of the lake. Campus police say they found the young man, Allan Jarocki, after a search effort. He was found there after he had gone missing. His parents had called the college police to report that he had disappeared.
The newspaper report continues,
"He apparently called a friend saying that he didn't know where he was. Authorities believe he was confused...."

In the same lake, Mike Knoll's body was found, "half-in and half-out of the water." He had been celebrating his birthday in a Bar in town with his college friends. It was just after 11.30pm when he walked out of the Bar. He'd been drinking but he wasn't thought by his friends to have been drunk, but for some indefinable reason he wandered into an old lady's home. She asked him what he was doing and he quickly left her house; she said he seemed confused and disoriented. His body was found four months later in the frozen Half Moon Lake. He was half-in and half- out of the water.

Where had he been in all those months? The lake had been searched thoroughly several times when he disappeared. His body had no signs of injury. The location was no-where near to where he lived nor where he had been drinking.

Back in 1997, in Wisconsin, nineteen year old Richard Hlavaty was tragically drowned after being chased into the river with his older brother, in an attempt to flee from a group of unidentified men. Their only safe refuge was to be the thing that killed him. His brother managed to survive and climb back out of the water once their pursuers had gone, but for this young man, driven into the water in terror, he failed to make it back to the shore and he died in the water.

As another victim's father says, is it a case that some of the victims are literally scared into the water; seeing no alternative when faced with violence by unknown attackers?

Allan Radell says, "I believe predators are preying on students who are leaving bars. Scot seemed to be disoriented. There were three phone calls back and forth, but Scot seemed to going the wrong way."

He was speaking out about the cases after his own son was found drowned, and what he suggested could have happened to his son, and many of the other men, is

harrowing, and highly sinister. He accepts that his son could have been intoxicated; however, it's what he thinks happened to him next that is so chilling;
"I think he got into a vehicle, voluntarily or not voluntarily. At some point, I believe he realized he was in trouble. He was a pretty tough kid, being a wrestler, but he was disoriented and vulnerable. Once he recognized what was going on, I think he managed to get away and ran in fear."

"Maybe he didn't know where he was going, or even that he was going toward the river. When he got to the bank, he didn't want to go back toward who he was running from. Directly across the river is a lighted stairway. He heads toward it not realizing there was water ahead of him. He goes in the water and swims as far as he could. He was a terrific swimmer; very strong, but it was cold, he had shoes on. He swam until he couldn't swim anymore."

On February 2, 2006, his son, Scott, had left one Bar in his University town, to go to meet his roommates at another bar, a few blocks away. It appears that he was at that point disoriented, as he went in the opposite direction to where the Bar was. During this walk he called his friends several times asking for directions to the Bar. Then his phone went dead. He never made it to the Bar. Later, investigators found what they thought were his footprints near the River's edge which appeared to show that he had been running.

What no-one can understand is how he got so disoriented. He and his friends had not been out in the Bar all that long. They also can't understand why he would have walked past busy streets full of Bars and then headed in the opposite direction from the Bars, and his campus. If he wasn't being chased and had accidentally found himself in freezing cold water, he would have got out of it pretty quickly. He didn't. Tracks show he had been running. He kept on swimming. He swam until he couldn't swim anymore.
What happened to him that night? Why was he so confused and disoriented? Why did his tracks show he had been running?

His body was found in the river a month later. It's entirely possible he was simply very drunk and walked into the water and drowned; his father however doesn't think it adds up to a lot of sense, and when comparing it to so many similar cases, I'm very much inclined to believe him.

In January 2014, a yacht was pulling up alongside a dock in Gastown, Vancouver. The propulsion of its propellers inadvertently dislodged something that was stuck beneath the dock. It was a young man's body. The coroner's report states that the manner of the person's death was undetermined. It explains that the large yacht dislodged the body under the dock.

When the forensic pathologist examined the body found, it was determined that there was a significant amount of post-mortem period of immersion in the water. In other words, it seemed that the body had been in the water for some time. The post-mortem also showed that there was no evidence of any trauma to the body. Due to the degree of decomposition however, it was also not possible to determine the manner in which the person came to be in the water nor what circumstance caused his death.

The coroner's report states "Due to post-mortem changes, and the incomplete nature of the remains, it is not possible to state definitely how he came to be in the waters, or what caused his death."

What struck a lot of people who knew the area well however, was how a body could have been there in the water for so long without it becoming dislodged sooner; it was a very busy water-way and harbour.

The body was that of Matthew Huszar, who had gone missing on the evening of December 16th, 2011, after attending a Christmas party. The location was Gastown, Vancouver, Canada. He had left the party at a Bar called the Lamplighter Pub on Water Street, and the last image of him is from surveillance footage at a bank machine. The geology graduate was discovered in the water; a distance of about 1.7 km from the bar he had been to.

What couldn't be explained either was how it had taken so long for his body to be found. Why would it take more than two years for a boat to dislodge his body, when boats moored there all the time? Was his body really there all that time? Or was it placed there? His body showed signs of having been in water for a period of time, but, as in the case of Chris Jenkins, whose body was moved several times to different areas of water, was this also the case for Matthew?

Newspapers in Canada reported, "Coroner Barb McLintock says it's still unknown how and why he reached the marina, two kilometres away, and in the opposite direction from his home."

According to a website set up by his family at the time of his disappearance, the young man was described by them as having no known problems in his life, no known mental health issues, and no substance abuse issues. He was not drunk on the night he disappeared, but toxicology tests after he was found did find traces of cocaine. They were at 'non-lethal' levels, meaning, it was not this which killed or contributed to his death, though he could have been 'fed' the drug. Gilbertson and Gannon did find that from independent toxicology reports done on some of the young men, they had various sedative drugs in their systems; pills which had never been prescribed to the victims, nor were they ever known to take such medication. Matthew was never known to have taken that drug either.

The young man's friends at the Christmas party stated that he was not drunk when he was with them, and that he was in a great mood. He had told his Mother that day that he was excited to be spending Christmas with his family. An avid outdoorsman, he was described as having a passion for climbing, camping and water sports.

Strangely, again, a cursory keyword search online, using the words this time; 'Matthew Huszar taken,' led to a search result which read;
'matthew huszar left an office dinner party Friday night in.....'
The words when clicked on led to a website called 'gematrix.org'
The site is a 'Gematria calculator.' Any words can be typed into the search bar on the site and it will then automatically calculate the numerical value of those words; which can then be used as 'a Kabbalistic method of interpreting the Hebrew bible scriptures.'

The complete search result said; "*matthew huszar* left an office dinner party friday night in gastown ...Universal Consciousness...we know, jump by your will or be *taken* by force. 7620 ..."
The beginning part of the message is copied from the headlines of a Newspaper report about the missing man. The origin of the second part is not known.
What is the person who typed this second part trying to say; Yes, we know what you are doing to these boys? They are being forced into the water; by being given two very chilling and horrific options? Either they go

into the water 'willingly,' 'voluntarily', to drown (although we all know this is not voluntary) or they will be forced into the water and drowned.

Again, this is most likely going looking at things way too deeply, seeing false leads and meaningless synchronicities? Quite possibly; but someone was 'interested' enough in the case of Matthew Huszar to type those words into the 'calculator' to look for its biblical meaning. Why was that?

Conclusion

In Boston, Zacharry Marr is still missing. The police said "it appears the surveillance images capture him entering the water." They have not, and probably will not be releasing this surveillance footage to the general public, and since they have searched the water again without finding him, there has been no more news coverage. It has all gone quite.

The day the police released this statement they searched the water thoroughly with divers, but they did not find him. What does not make any sense is the reason why this Harvard graduate would even consider entering the water; ice cold water, late at night, when he had only stepped outside a Pub that was not located beside the water, to smoke a cigarette?

It's almost identical in its 'modus operandi'...the Pub, the disappearance while out with friends, and the body not being found for some time...just like all the other cases.

The hope is that he is found safe, alive, and well. The hope is that he does not become another of the statistics...that this is all an exaggeration, that it is all the product of overactive imaginations....that this is not really happening at all...that it is individual cases where circumstances have somehow caused them to disappear, that is unrelated....that it is not connected....that we have got it wrong....but it's the same water where Mathew Genovese, Dennis Njoroge, Eric Munsell, David Dreher, and Anthony Urena have recently been found.

"Once so vital, he is now...grist for the mill. For a machine...A machine full of teeth...he never saw coming."

"If people knew the depth of this, they would be terrified to be outside at night, whether out in the country or in the city."

Also by Steph Young
(writing as Stephen Young)

Something in the Woods is Taking People

Hunted in the Woods

Taken in the Woods

Predators in the Woods

Mysterious Things in the Woods

Terror in the Night

Monsters in the Dark

Encounters with the Unknown

True stories of Real Time Travelers

Made in the USA
Charleston, SC
09 June 2016